LEARNING

THEOLOGY

FROM THE

THIRD WORLD

LEARNING
ABOUT
THEOLOGY
FROM THE
THIRD WORLD

WILLIAM A. DYRNESS

Academie
Books Grand Rapids, Michigan
Zondervan Publishing House

Learning About Theology From The Third World
Copyright © 1990 by William A. Dyrness

Academie Books is an imprint of Zondervan Publishing House,
1415 Lake Drive, S.E., Grand Rapids, Michigan 49506.

Library of Congress Cataloging in Publication Data

Dyrness, William A.
    Learning about theology from the Third World / William A. Dyrness.
        p.   cm.
    Includes bibliographical references.
    ISBN 0-310-20971-4
    1. Theology, Doctrinal—Developing countries—History—20th
century.   2.Theology—Methodology.   3. Christianity and culture.
4. Developing countries—Church history—20th century.   I. Title.
BT30.D44D96   1990
230'.09172'4—dc20   90-31260
                                                               CIP

All Scripture quotations, unless otherwise noted, are taken from the HOLY
BIBLE: NEW INTERNATIONAL VERSION (North American Edition). Copyright © 1973, 1978, 1984, by the International Bible Society. Used by
permission of Zondervan Bible Publishers.

Edited by Gerard Terpstra

Printed in the United States of America

90 91 92 93 94 / CH / 10 9 8 7 6 5 4 3 2 1

To
Modupe
and
Olive Taylor-Pearce,
beloved brother and sister in Christ

CONTENTS

Preface vii

1 **Introduction** 11
The Rise of the Third World 11
How Is the Third World Defined? 14
Evangelicalism and Third World Theology 17
Is There Any Cross-cultural Theory? 20
How Does Scripture Relate to a Particular Context? ... 24

2 **African Theology: Christianity and Culture** 35
The Agenda of African Theology 35
Historical Setting of African Theology 36
What Is the African Worldview? 42
Basic Elements of an African Worldview 43
Theological Perspectives 52
Conclusion: Toward an African Christianity
Rooted in Culture 63

3 **Latin American Theology: Christianity
and Its Political Setting** 71
Introduction: Why Is There Such Misery? 71
Background and Development of
Liberation Theology 75
A New Way of Doing Theology? 86
Some Theological Issues 99
What Have We Learned From Liberation Theology? ... 111

4 **Asian Theology: Christianity
and the Transcendent** 121
The Asian Context 121
India and Sri Lanka and the Theology
of the Person 126

China and the Question of History 135
Japan and the Nature of Spirituality 141
Philippines and Southeast Asia 150
Conclusion: What Have We Learned From Asia? 155

5 **Christology: A Cross-cultural Study** 163
Africa: Christ and the Ancestors 166
Latin America: Christ and Political Power 170
Asia: Christ and the Transcendent 175
Summary 180

6 **Where Do We Go From Here?** 185
Who Sees Things Whole? 185
The Third World and Renewal 188
Is the West at the End of Its History? 190
The Third World and Modernization:
What Role Will Theology Play? 192

Bibliography 197

Index 213

PREFACE

This book is meant to give a general introduction to the way Christians outside of Europe and North America think about their faith. A book of such an ambitious scope is bound to raise eyebrows, in some cases even blood pressure. For not only are we attempting to deal with a bewildering variety of peoples and cultures, we are also delving into matters that are often politically sensitive. Even the choice of the designation "Third World" rather than "Two-Thirds World" or "Three-Fourths World" appears derogatory to some people. (I have made this particular choice because "Third World" was the original name the nonaligned nations chose for themselves in the 1950s, and it is widely understood.)

What can be gained by attempting such a broad overview? The main response to this question, and my fundamental motivation for writing the book, is that a simple—even oversimplified—idea of what is going on in other parts of the world is infinitely better than no idea at all. For it is not hard to show that Western Christians ordinarily have only the vaguest idea of what their counterparts in other parts of the world are thinking. This book, offered with generous apologies, is meant to introduce and stimulate interest in these other parts of the Christian world.

A further defense lies in the advantages offered by a comparative study of the differing emphases of the various regions of the world. Indian theologian Ken Gnanakan has argued that the day of cross-cultural evangelism in many places is giving way to intracultural evangelism. The corollary of this is that local reflection on Scripture and faith is producing a variety of perspectives on theology. Studying some of these in a comparative way will surely enrich theological discussion and, when Scripture is allowed to be the final authority, may help correct some of the excesses to which we all are prone. The goal I will argue is that this will stimulate us all to think more carefully about our faith in our own setting.

I would even dare to go further and argue that cross-cultural theology—that is, theology that studies theological traditions in their cultural and historical setting—will be one of the most important enterprises of theological study in the decades ahead. The chapter on Christology in this book is meant to be a tentative case study of the direction such comparative study might take.

Still a major limitation of this study will inevitably be its general and simplified character. This is especially true because I believe, as I argue in the first chapter, that the more specific the interaction between Scripture and its cultural setting can be, the more fruitful will be the results. But the reader should bear this limitation in mind, excusing it perhaps as necessary to an introductory study of this kind.

Without a large amount of outside encouragement added to a large measure of audacity, this discussion would not have proceeded very far. Here I acknowledge those discussion partners who taught me much of what I know. Colleagues at Asian Theological Seminary in Manila, especially Dr. David Lim and Professor Lorenzo Bautista, first showed me the limitation of my perspectives and taught me what it means to think differently about God. I am especially grateful to the students in my Third World Theology class at the Nairobi Evangelical Graduate School of Theology during the spring of 1989 for helping me refine some of the argument: Douglas Carew, Oscar Muriu, Omar Djoeandy, James Nkansah-Obrem-pong, Kingsley Larbi, Mateso Akou, and Johnson Rogho. I am further indebted to Mutava Musyimi, Ken R. Gnanakan, Joel B. Green, Thomas Gledhill, and Chester Wood, all of whom read and commented on various parts of the manuscript. Allen

Flemming gave much appreciated help on the index. The debt I owe to my wife, Grace, and my father-in-law, W. Dayton Roberts, for helping me understand Latin America, is considerable. Dayton's deep understanding of liberation theology has been especially valuable.

Finally, I must thank Principal Modupe Taylor-Pearce and his wife, Olive, of NEGST in Nairobi, for their wonderful hospitality and especially for their Christian love and friendship. This book is dedicated to them as a small token of our family's love for them and our gratitude to the entire NEGST family. It is clearly their prayer and ours that God be exalted among the nations!

Berkeley, California
October 1989

1

INTRODUCTION

After this I looked and there before me was a great multitude that no one could count, from every nation, tribe, people and language, standing before the throne and in front of the Lamb. They were wearing white robes and were holding palm branches in their hands. And they cried out in a loud voice: "Salvation belongs to our God, who sits on the throne, and to the Lamb." All the angels were standing around the throne and around the elders and the four living creatures. They fell down on their faces before the throne and worshiped God, saying: "Amen! Praise and glory and wisdom and thanks and honor and power and strength be to our God for ever and ever. Amen!" Revelation 7:9–12

THE RISE OF THE THIRD WORLD

When I was growing up in Illinois, most of what I knew about what is now called the Third World came from returned missionaries. During long Sunday evening services they would show slides of mud huts and talk about people who seemed to have little in common with me. It never occurred to me that what happened in those strange areas of the world had any real relevance for me or people I knew. In this, I suppose, I was much like most of my contemporaries, whose primary contact with that other world was via *National Geographic* magazines. When I went away to seminary in the late 1960s I learned about theology and the history of the church. But outside of our missions classes nothing that happened in this other world was considered of real significance. Any theology worthy of the name came from Germany, the Netherlands, or Britain, and, now and then, from America. If there was theological reflection taking place in other parts of the world, we knew nothing about it.

Today, while there is still much ignorance about the Third World, there is a growing awareness of the interconnectedness of peoples and nations. Not only is it possible to travel to every corner of the world in a few hours, but events in these places are seen to be signficant in world terms. Famines, earthquakes, and unrest in one part of the world, we are coming to see, inevitably have effects elsewhere. Rioting on the West Bank, oil strikes in Africa, or drug trafficking in South America are watched with interest not only by diplomats or financiers, but by almost everyone. The question I would like to ask in this study is this: Has this world setting signficantly affected the way we Christians in the West think about our faith? Have we made the connection between economic and political relations and theological exchange?

This challenge was brought home to me during one of the last years our family lived as missionaries in the Philippines in the early 1980s. Each spring missionaries from our mission gathered for a planning conference. The speaker at this particular meeting was one of the older respected Filipino leaders who was brought to Christ, recruited, and trained by the people he was talking to. At the end of his message he told us something that must have been very difficult for a soft-spoken, modest Filipino to say to Western missionaries. The situation of missions was changing, he had been telling us, and the need for new relations was urgent. In conclusion he summarized the situation as he saw it: "We have had the privilege of being dependent on you. Now we would like you to have the privilege of being dependent on us."

Many events of the last generation made such a shift possible and, many would argue, necessary. Following World War II, during the so-called Cold War, many of the newly independent countries refused to line up behind the communist East or the capitalist West. In 1955 representatives of twenty-nine of these countries met at the famous Bandung

Conference, the first of many conferences of "nonaligned" nations. It was there the term "Third World" was born, as a description of this new politically independent section of the world.

Accompanying this growing political maturity, and arguably one of its causes, has been a rapidly growing Christian church in the Third World, a church that has come to overshadow that in the West. In 1900, for example, Christians in Latin America, Africa, and Asia numbered a mere 86.7 million, compared to 333.2 million in Europe and North America. By 1988 Third World Christians numbered 826.6 million, compared to 594.7 in the West. Indeed it is hard to overemphasize the importance of this growing and maturing part of Christendom. Professor A. F. Walls, of the University of Aberdeen, puts such changes in these terms:

> One of the most important . . . events in the whole of Christian history, has occurred within the lifetime of people not yet old. It has not reached the textbooks, and most Christians, including many of the best informed, do not know it has happened. It is nothing less than a complete change in the centre of gravity of Christianity, so that the heartlands of the Church are no longer in Europe, decreasingly in North America, but in Latin America, in certain parts of Asia, and . . . in Africa. (1976:180)

Professor Walls goes on to draw a conclusion from this that is important for the thesis of this book. If it is true that theology that matters will be a theology of the majority of Christians, then "theology in the Third World is now the only theology worth caring about" (182). If theology is to be rooted in the actual lives of Christians today, increasingly it will have to be from the poor to the poor, in Africa, Latin America, and Asia. And theology done in the West, if it is not to become increasingly provincial, he notes, will have to be done in dialogue with the theological leaders in the Third World.

For our part, if we are able to distance ourselves from the noise and heat generated by the theological battles of the West—not an easy thing for us to do—we will find that an increasingly sophisticated theological discussion is being carried on in the Third World. Already in 1966 the All-Africa Conference of Churches met in Ibadan, Nigeria, and produced important reflections on Christianity in an African setting (see Dickson and Ellingworth, 1971). In 1976 in Dar es Salaam, Tanzania, the Ecumenical Association of Third World theologians was born (see Torres and Fabella, 1978), and it has become an important forum for theological reflection. As we will note, evangelicals have been slower to encourage such reflection, but hopeful signs are appearing here as well. In the 1970s fraternities of evangelical Theologians were formed in Latin America, Asia, and Africa and have sponsored important conferences (see Gitari and Benson, 1986; Samuel and Sugden, 1983). It is significant that the theological commission of the World Evangelical Fellowship along with the Lausanne Committee has encouraged important discussion on these issues (see Nicholls, 1979; Stott and Coote, 1980).

HOW IS THE THIRD WORLD DEFINED?

Our concern in this book, then, is with theology coming from that part of the world that is called the Third (or more recently the Two-Thirds) World, consisting of Latin America, Africa, and South and Southeast Asia. Before going further it is fair to ask whether it is possible to make meaningful generalizations about an area so large and so diverse.

This vast section of the world, making up three-fourths of the world's population, is a kaleidoscope of cultures and traditions. Even so, it has many common characteristics that distinguish it from its northern and southern neighbors (see Paul Harrison, *Inside the Third World*).

In the first place, a large portion of the people of this region are poor. The World Bank estimated in 1980 that the number of people unable to afford the basic WHO/FAO—recommended diet was 750 million, or one person in three in the noncommunist developing countries (ibid., 462). This situation is aggravated by widespread shortages of medical and educational facilities and even more basic social services. As a result Third World literature and art reflect a concrete and continuing struggle to survive hardships with dignity. Overpopulation (or, less often, the reverse), hostile physical environments, and an unrelenting tropical sun, among other factors, conspire to make life for most people of the Third World an unceasing struggle.

Second, these countries have all survived unequal and sometimes debilitating relations with the richer northern countries (which I will ordinarily call the West in this study), relations that have left their mark in the form of economic and cultural dependencies and inequities. Ali Mazrui notes, "The bonds between Africa and Asia include the experience of racial humiliation as non-white people. The bonds between Africa and Latin America include the experience of exploitation" (1980:xi). As newly formed nations struggle to find their own identity, there is often, quite understandably, suspicion or outright rejection of Western influences. At the same time there is a desperate need for external capital to finance infrastructure (roads and communication facilities) and an industrial base.

Third, all three of these areas were once the home of sophisticated civilizations and religious traditions. In Latin America the Inca and Maya civilizations equaled and surpassed some of the technical and political achievements in the West. The Sudanic and Chinese civilizations, in Africa and Asia, were in advance of contemporary civilizations in the West in many respects. India is the home of some of the richest religious traditions of the world. Today, in a world where rules are made somewhere else, these countries struggle to maintain the integrity of their traditions and a continuity with their past. Memory is very important to a people, and much of modern history has had the effect of eliminating or belittling such memories in the Third World. Both Marxism and capitalism, each in its own way, have communicated that the history of these regions reflects weakness and failures that must be overcome if the people are to enter the modern world. Consequently many people in these countries feel that they are forced to lose their soul in order to come to terms with the developed world.

Fourth, the peoples of these areas share a deeply religious outlook on life. Often nourished by their ancient and deeply rooted traditions, they treasure the spiritual and mystical dimensions of life. As a result, though they are sometimes slow in appreciating the technical skills of the modern world, they possess profound skills in fostering interpersonal relations and family and alliance systems.

These issues, and others I have not listed, characterize the Third World as a whole. Accordingly, theology emanating from this part of the world will in some ways reflect and engage the issues of poverty, indigenous and modernizing traditions, and cultural and family pride. But the way these issues are addressed will reflect the unique history and culture of each region (and even each ethnic group).

In this study I will be arguing that each of the three major regions of the Third World has a distinctive way of responding to these issues and thus a special way of reading Scripture and formulating the Gospel. While neat boundaries are not possible, I will argue there are distinctive styles that Latin American, Asian, and African people reflect in thinking about Christianity (just as there is a distinctive style we Americans bring to our faith; see Dyrness, 1989).

Let me try to summarize these styles in an introductory way. African theologians tend to focus on the way Christianity relates to particular cultural forms and ask how the Gospel can be expressed in terms of these traditions. All peoples have cultural forms, but no people have been so preoccupied with how their rich cultural traditions provide a warrant for the values of the Gospel as have African theologians. Latin American theologians, because of the political oppression they have suffered and their resultant underdevelopment, have tended to focus on the political dimensions of poverty and the struggle to preserve cultural integrity. For reasons we will explore, they have tended to find in their own history political dynamics that urgently call for resolution. All peoples organize themselves into political groupings, but for various reasons

Latin American Christians tend to see this dimension as a key to understanding the values of the kingdom. Asian theologians, by contrast, have sought to relate their faith to religious values, especially as these are found in the ancient and ever-present traditions of the major religions (Buddhism and Hinduism). As a result they have reflected more on the religious and philosophical nature of reality than others have. Their questions often relate to what we might call the transcendent dimension of life.

Although these are common elements that Third World writers themselves have pointed out, they are nevertheless broad (and perhaps foolhardy) generalizations. They call for a great deal of clarification and support, but they are offered here as a part of a broader thesis that each style of doing theology, and therefore each people, has its own particular contribution to make to our full understanding of God's Word. Paul writes in Ephesians 4 that we are all—Africans, Latin Americans, Asians, Americans—reaching maturity in Christ together. Christ has given us all gifts "to prepare God's people for works of service, so that the body of Christ may be built up until we all reach unity in the faith and in the knowledge of the Son of God" (Eph. 4:12–13). Each group will in some way distort the truth of Scripture, but because of the universal created gifts of God and the presence of his Holy Spirit, each will see a special part of the truth that others might miss. Presently we will want to elaborate this complementarity further, but first we must face another question.

EVANGELICALISM AND THIRD WORLD THEOLOGY

We have noted that evangelicals came late to discussions of Third World theology. Since this book is written from an evangelical point of view this fact needs further discussion. For our purposes an evangelical will be defined as one who holds that the truth of God's revelation given in Scripture is transcultural and therefore the final authority in theology. This

Word of God of course must be heard and received in terms of some particular culture. The latter process is what we call "doing theology": reading and reflecting on God's Word in the context of a particular culture. What is primary and determinative is the Word of God, though this is always heard and construed in terms given by some culture (see on this whole issue the important essays in Stott and Coote, 1980).

Other theologians—some of whom we will study in this book—take as their reference point the context or life situation of the interpreter as in some way primary to Scripture. These emphasize the fact that God is already present in all cultures, and that he is everywhere working out his purposes. Our work as theologians, then, is to discern what he is doing and read that in the light of the Gospel. The difference between the two points of view seems straightforward: The evangelical is anxious to translate what God is saying into terms a culture will understand; the other culturally oriented theologian wants to see what God is up to in a given situation as this is illuminated by the Gospel.

Although our sympathies are clearly with the evangelical, issues do not always sort themselves out as simply as we would like. In the first place the evangelical church in most parts of the world has been a church without a theology. In many places missionaries and evangelists worked for years before starting theological seminaries. When these were formed, they usually were conceived to "train pastors and Christian workers" rather than to be a center of theological reflection. There have clearly been advantages to this set of priorities, as church growth among evangelicals in the last generation indicates. But a weakness has been the absence, until recently, of serious and sustained biblical and theological reflection on issues facing the church. Happily this situation is now changing rapidly; however, the initiative in theological reflection has been with more liberally oriented theologians.

As a result most of the theology one reads from the Third World would not be classed as "evangelical," though among these writings there is much careful and sensitive reflection being done. We have noted the absence until recently of a theological sense among evangelicals in the Third World. But it is also safe to say that those who take Scripture as authoritative often fail to add anything substantial to theology because they do not take their context with sufficient seriousness. Samuel Escobar had this problem in mind when he said:

> When theological formulas are made sacred which are forged in other latitudes and with respect to other questions and there is a hesitance to read afresh the word of God itself, to search out its message, it is worth nothing to have a correct theory about the authority of Scripture. (1987:170)

On the other hand, many times those whose theory of Scripture may seem deficient, by dint of sensitive listening to the context, strike a note that is more biblical than those with the better "theory." Our method, then, will be one of openness to theologians from many points of view, not necessarily to correct them but rather to learn from them. For our search is to discover what is characteristic about theologians from the major areas of the world. It will certainly be necessary to point out what, from our point of view, appear to be the weaknesses of various emphases. But we will note also the strengths that their perspectives give them. In either case we will have something to learn.

As Samuel Escobar implied, we must at all costs avoid giving the sense that these theologies must all be judged and corrected from any one particular point of view, which for us usually turns out to be Western. Of course Scripture has the right to judge any and all theologies, and we will surely speak out when we believe Scripture is clear. But we will notice that the emphases of one "regional theology," when compared with those of another, tend to correct the other—the strengths of one illuminate the weaknesses of the other.

Nor is it supposed, despite the hyperbole of Professor Walls, that Third World theology is the only thing worth studying today. It is true that many of the creative movements of theology since World War II have come from the non-Western world, as we will see. But the issues with which Western theologies struggle—technology, medical ethics, secularism, feminism, the environment and so on—are all issues that are of growing importance in the Third World. In fact, we will argue that the all-pervasive question that Third World theologies fail to deal with in any significant way, modernization, is precisely the point at which Western theologies may make their best contribution.

All of this suggests that any theology today that claims to be comprehensive must result from an interchange between theologians from many different settings and representing many different points of view. Those of us who take the authority of Scripture seriously would add that only through such interchange will the full truth of Scripture be seen.

IS THERE ANY CROSS-CULTURAL THEORY?

I have spoken about my concern that theology formed in one part of the world not be allowed to dictate a perspective for another part. But this concern leads me to ask: How do we think about theology cross-culturally? Or to put this in more fundamental (or philosophical) terms: Is cross-cultural theology possible?

Here we are dealing with two fears: the first is the fear of *ethnocentrism*. Following the rise to prominence of the social sciences, educated people in the West have become very conscious of the fact that we often assume that our way of doing things is the only correct way. Basically this has to do with the power of definition. When we define what theology is, or ought to be, we can easily, and unconsciously, assume that our definition is universally valid. Hidden in this, of course, is the assumption that our ways of understanding are superior to others'.

This fear has led in some cases to an opposite danger, which we might call xenocentrism. That is, we might be so afraid of dictating to others, that we begin by assuming that our ways of thinking are invariably false and in need of correction from outside. In this case we might go to other cultures assuming that they are superior to ours (after all, their divorce rate or suicide rate is probably lower than ours, and they look so happy). As Clifford Geertz warns, we must avoid believing foreign wisdom "is a prosthetic corrective for a damaged spirituality" (1983:44).

In both these cases the danger is the same: taking our point of view too seriously, either as invariably right or invariably wrong. It is difficult to see how someone in this situation can properly evaluate and profit from another's point of view.

But there is a second fear that we must reckon with: the fear of *relativism*. Evangelicals especially are suspicious of any position that seems to assume that anybody's point of view is as good as anyone else's. We are committed to the fact that God has given his revelation in a form that carries universal validity, so we cannot say that all cultural views are equally true.

Anthropologists are sometimes accused of encouraging this view as a deterrent against missionaries' attempts to "convert the natives." But in actual fact only a minority of social scientists would insist on this hard relativism. Philosopher Charles Taylor discusses this view, which he calls the incorrigibility thesis, in an important article on cross-cultural knowledge (1985:121–25). He acknowledges that one must take the native's point of view into account, when, for example, one tries to understand a ritual act. But it does not follow from this that the native's point of view is perfectly adequate, or that it cannot be corrected from outside.

The error, he explains, is to assume that cross-cultural theory has to be either ours or theirs, that is, that it must be either ethnocentric or incorrigible. Taylor suggests a middle way that he calls the interpretive view. This position seeks to find a way of understanding and description that challenges both the observer's and the native's self-understanding. He argues that by challenging the native's language of self-understanding as an outsider, we are also challenging ours (indeed he feels that we cannot really question one without questioning the other).

It could be, then, that an adequate language with which to understand another point of view, would be neither theirs nor ours, but "a language in which we could formulate both their way of life and ours as alternative possibilities in relation to some human constant at work in both" (ibid., 125). To apply this to theology, we might find that by describing both their way of reading Scripture and ours as alternative possibilities, we might find their language to be distorted or inadequate, or we might find ours, or, in fact, both to be so. This is another way of saying that a dialogue among theological views may be mutually corrective.

Christians believe that the human constant present in all cultures is the result of people's being created in God's image and is further illuminated in God's revelation in Scripture. Therefore analogies among cultures—and the "translation" of concepts from one cultural idiom to another—are possible. Recent anthropology and sociology, from this same "interpretive" point of view, have shown us the possibility of reshaping "categories (ours and other people's—think of 'taboo') so that they can reach beyond the contexts in which they originally arose and took their meaning so as to locate affinities and mark differences" (Clifford Geertz, 1983:12; see also Herbert Blumer, 1969). Out of such dialogue better understanding will surely arise.

Let us elaborate this point further in order to show its relevance for theology. In contemporary philosophy a great deal of discussion is concerned with the nature of theory (the general ideas that people use to guide their thinking and behavior). We now believe that theory is not only theory of a disinterested "objective" observer but also a part of a communal self-definition. It is, in other words, not only about our practices but also a part of those practices, an essential part of the way we put our world together. Theology, which is a particular kind of theory, may then be understood as a part of the communal self-definition and practice that make a believing community what it is.

Further, we are becoming increasingly aware, as I have argued above, that communities, no less than individuals, are interdependent. Benjamin Nelson (1981) has argued, for example, that, by virtue of the interconnectedness of the modern world, all present and future knowledge will necessarily be cross-cultural. A moment's thought will show that all the major issues we face—the environment, the arms race, international indebtedness, social and cultural dislocation, AIDS—are essentially cross-cultural issues. Accordingly, they will not be properly addressed from a parochial point of view.

Since we live in a world of common or interrelated practices, our understanding needs a broader "horizon" than we have given it heretofore in the West. To take but one example, which will occupy us at length below, in Western theology, due to our philosophical heritage, we have tended to define God abstractly: What is his nature and how is he to be defined? The Christian life is then often defined in terms of similar abstract qualities—the "deeper life" or "victorious living." This method has become congenial to us and has facilitated our comprehension of Scripture. Many Africans, however, experience life in terms of concrete dilemmas—Why is the child sick? Why aren't the crops healthy? As a result they tend to think of God in terms of what he does; they are concerned with his power rather than his nature. Latin Americans, by contrast, ask about God's interest and involvement in the political process. Latin theologians are asking us to "open an horizon of interpretation in which politics is understood as the comprehensive and decisive sphere in which Christian truth should become praxis" (D. Soelle, 1974:59). It could be that a genuine dialogue between these points of view will suggest language that will challenge both their point of view and ours.

Since theory (and theology) is not of a detached observer, but of an agent and participant, and these agents are inextricably interrelated, it is now necessary to broaden the scope of those participating in the theological discussion. This is reason enough to study Third World theology, just as it has encouraged us to listen to minority voices in our midst. Too often our theology, like our history, has been written by the winners, at least those with resources and ready access to means of communication. Perhaps a better perspective will be gained by giving a voice to those who are the victims of the injustices of a fallen world and who to this point have remained silent. As Martin Luther put it, it is not reading and writing that makes a theologian, but living and dying and being damned.

HOW DOES SCRIPTURE RELATE TO A PARTICULAR CONTEXT?

For Christians there is a more important reason for believing that cross-cultural theology is possible: We believe that God has created the world and intervened through a series of events, focusing on the death and resurrection of Christ, to redeem that world after it had fallen away from his purposes. These facts are relevant, indeed essential, to all people everywhere, and they are preserved in an authoritative way in Scripture.

Of course the hard part is to describe how this message relates to particular cultures, an issue that has come to be called "contextualization." Since this relationship is implied throughout this study, we must try to sketch here some guidelines that we will use to think about theology around the world. To remind ourselves that this is an issue that has to be faced by actual believers in concrete situations, let us begin with a story (adapted from Hiebert and Hiebert, 1987:126–28).

In a remote village in India ravaged by a plague of smallpox a Christian "untouchable," Venkayya, is facing a major decision. The village diviner has determined that the goddess of smallpox, who lives under a tree outside the village, is offended and must be appeased by the sacrifice of a water buffalo. So the high caste village elders begin a collection from the villagers for the sacrifice. They are very angry when Venkayya refuses to give to the collection, and they bar him from the village lands and water. Children continue to die, and in fact Venkayya's own daughter becomes ill. What should he do? Has his God abandoned him? Should he give to the sacrifice even if he doesn't believe in it so that he can work his lands? Or should he stand firm in his faith?

The answers one would give to these questions depend on

a great many factors. But the major factor is the picture that Venkayya has in his mind of the way his faith relates to his culture. Even though he has probably not thought about it much, the way he has learned the Gospel and his experience with God (and other Christians) have probably given him a rough picture of this relationship. Let us propose four different models of the way the Gospel relates to culture and see how these would influence Venkayya to respond to his situaion (the first three models are discussed with others in Bevans, 1985:185–202).

The first model we might call the *anthropological model*, since it implies a thorough understanding and appreciation of culture. This view is represented by the Asian theologian Choan-Seng Song, whom we will discuss in some detail below. Beginnning with the confidence that comes from knowing that God is creator and sustainer of the whole world, Song assumes that God is present in all cultures and is working out his purposes. Thus all peoples and their history display the struggle of God with the forces of evil, a struggle particularly displayed in the work of Christ. Moreover, it is the history as lived by the common person struggling with the forces of evil (rather than that of the highly educated observer) that displays most clearly what God is up to.

Starting with these assumptions, Venkayya might see the struggle of his village with this plague as an instance of God's struggle with evil throughout history. These people in their own way are seeking to come to terms with evil and find God, their search has an integrity that must be respected. Venkayya's love for his village, then, may well suggest to him that he contribute to the collection, while he points out to them that God is deeply concerned about their plight and in fact has shown his concern in the death of Christ.

But, despite Song's concern to listen respectfully to what God is doing and to give an important place to Christ's work, we may wonder if this model takes either the death of Christ or the culture with sufficient seriousness. In the first place is Christ's work simply an instance of God's struggle with evil, or is it the locus of a final and victorious encounter between the two? Clearly Christ's work does illumine our own struggles, but only because a decisive blow was struck there against evil, the strong man was bound in such a way that we might be freed from his power. Second, does taking a culture seriously necessitate treating it uncritically? Perhaps belief in the spirits and the need for sacrifice is simply wrong. Does the Gospel not provide some leverage against the injustice and abuse that every culture displays? It is hard to see how it can if one approaches it in terms of this model.

Perhaps this weakness can be corrected by a second model, which we will call the *praxis model*, as it is represented by Latin American theologian Gustavo Gutiérrez (at least during his earliest writings). This view also wants to take culture seriously and so begins with an analysis of especially its socio-economic dimensions. Gutiérrez believes that such an analysis invariably uncovers basic contradictions that call for resolution. The urgency of the situation demands that we take sides on behalf of those who are oppressed, a response that is a prerequisite to any reflection on the Gospel. Reflection on this concrete struggle in terms of Scripture leads one to see that God's basic involvement in history is for liberation from all kinds of oppression.

Gutiérrez therefore would point out that there is a basic social contradiction inherent in Venkayya's situation, namely, his exploitation by the upper-caste elders and perhaps the exploitation of the village by a government that favors the rich. Gutiérrez might see as unrealistic and ultimately unworkable the seeking of a medical or religious solution outside of a larger framework of liberation (including political liberation). Such piecemeal solutions, he might argue, distract people from addressing the larger structural issues.

The attempt to broaden the horizon is helpful, but one wonders, in the light of the immediate demands being made on Venkayya, what a reasonable definition of liberation might be. And what if there is no realistic possibility of liberating action (i.e., what if his daughter dies?), what hope does the Gospel give? But this model has introduced the important category of practice as an essential component of theological insight, a virtue I will want to comment on later in our study.

Is there not some way to allow the Gospel to be placed within culture without changing its content? An evangelical view that seeks to preserve this character is what might be called the *translation model* as this is represented by American ethnotheologian Charles Kraft (see his *Christianity in Culture*, 1979). Kraft believes that though God is transcultural he communicates through culture. Although in a multicultural format, the Bible, which Kraft calls God's inspired casebook, has one message from beginning to end. The goal is to "decode" the message so that it can be re-encoded "within the hearer's frame of reference in such a way that both communication and response are dynamically equivalent to those of the original situation" (1979:282). Notice that the message is to be abstracted from its context in the biblical culture and put into new cultural forms with no change in its content. Kraft seems to assume that cultural forms are neutral with respect to the Gospel truth, which can be abstracted from its context in the biblical context: he uses the analogy of the water of the Gospel being poured through different "cultural" pipes (though he does insist that the Gospel will have its impact on the receptor culture).

The situation of Venkayya highlights a weakness of the translation model and its emphasis on the communication of truth, for Venkayya is called on not so much to formulate Christian truth in a new setting as to respond to a cultural challenge in a Christian way. Kraft may look on this encounter as an opportunity to present the Gospel in a form these villagers would relate to. But it is hard to see how any communication of Christian truth in this setting would meet the demands of the elders. Perhaps Kraft would feel that Christians should take the opportunity to organize their own service of prayer to call on God to deliver them from their misfortune on the basis of the sacrifice of Christ. This of course might result in a power encounter between the God of the Bible and the goddess of smallpox. Since healing and deliverance are what these people wish for, these are what Christianity ought to claim for its God.

But within the Indian worldview, would such a delivering event really be equivalent to the deliverance promised in Christ? Or would it simply be absorbed into their syncretistic worldview? Two problems are apparent here. First, it is not clear that bringing the Gospel is simply a matter of decoding and encoding a message. In its scriptural context the Good News is likened to the leaven of the new age permeating the dough of culture or to a binding of a strong man and ravaging his house. Nor is it easy to see how the message can be so easily isolated from its context in Scripture. Indeed I will argue in this book that it is Scripture, and not its "message," that is finally transcultural. Gospel after all means "good news" and what appears to one culture as good may not be good at all to another. For example, it does not sound like good news to a Hindu that we are "born again" in Christ, for the Hindu is trying to escape the tyrannical circle of rebirths to reach a state of final union with God. It might be that good news for this person is the final union that Christ makes possible with God—hardly a formulation that would appeal to middle-class Americans. Although it will surely relate in some fundamental way to Christ and his work, what is transcultural is not some core truth, but Scripture—the full biblical context of Christ's work. It is this that must be allowed to strike its own spark in the light of the needs of particular cultures.

The second problem is that cultural forms are rarely neutral with respect to the values of Scripture. Occasionally they oppose these values, at times they support them, more often they appear ambiguous. To use the metaphor of Kraft, cultural forms cannot be like pipes that allow the water of the Gospel to flow, for in many cases the shape of the pipes determines what will count as water! What makes Venkayya's decision difficult is that the forms he is immersed in are both social and religious; they demand not only social cohesion and respect, but also religious devotion. What shape will obedience take in this setting? Can it accommodate respect for the elders? The interplay between cultural elements and Scripture is apparently more complex than Kraft's model allows.

Can we propose a model that allows for this complexity and yet preserves the transformational character of God's word? The model I propose may be called the *interactional model* and is laid out in the diagram on the following page:

The process of contextualization begins when the missionary or evangelist proclaims the message of Scripture (which may in fact be contextualized to some other cultural setting). This preaching will certainly make some attempt to connect what Scripture says to cultural values, but this is not yet contextualized theology. What is commonly overlooked is that the impact comes often from the life as well as the message of the evangelist, for this will also speak to the situation of the hearer.

For the Gospel to be contextualized two things must occur: First, the Scripture must be read and obeyed by believers in this culture and, second, the culture must be opened by analysis. On the one hand the believer will read and respond to Scripture in the light of the questions the culture suggests. Here she or he will encounter dilemmas like that of Venkayya. These very dilemmas may lead to the second step: culture must be made to reveal its deep-seated needs and aspirations. Notice what is assumed here is that the questions of a culture, its needs and ambitions, are important to God. For God is already in the culture working out his purposes, but Scripture and the Good News of Scripture are not there; they must come from outside.

The believer, then, will respond to those themes of Scripture that parallel the questions of the culture. Everyone, of course, reads the Bible with certain presuppositions provided by his or her culture and personal needs, and it is important that this fact be acknowledged from the beginning. A failure to reckon with these assumptions may be one of the reasons that conversion does not bring as radical a transformation as we would like. As Indian theologian M. M. Thomas puts it:

Interactional Model of Contextualization

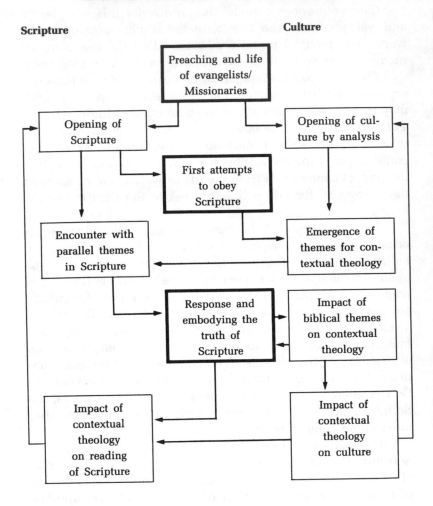

Scripture   Culture

Preaching and life
of evangelists/
Missionaries

Opening of
Scripture

Opening of cul-
ture by analysis

First attempts
to obey
Scripture

Encounter with
parallel themes
in Scripture

Emergence of
themes for con-
textual theology

Response and
embodying the
truth of
Scripture

Impact of
biblical themes
on contextual
theology

Impact of
contextual
theology
on reading
of Scripture

Impact of
contextual
theology
on culture

Adapted from
R. Schreiter (1985:25)

30

Where a people's pre-understanding is left alone without bringing it under the service of the Christian Gospel (believers) will remain pre-Christian in their mind and this will affect the whole person in due course. Their response to the Christian faith, being unrelated to their inner thought patterns, will remain limited and immature. (1969:303)

But how are these patterns brought under the service of the Gospel? Only by a serious interaction with Scripture. When parallel themes emerge from Scripture, they will also have their own impact on the growing understanding of the believer. But notice, as the boxes in bold lines imply, this will take place only as the truth of Scripture begins to take root in the lives of Christians. This is a vital part of the process of growth; indeed, it is a part of the reflection process itself. The values of culture and its questions may be affirmed, but they will also be challenged by new values and a larger perspective. And out of this interaction, which is sometimes called a hermeneutical circle, comes a genuinely contextualized theology.

Here I underline the importance of my conviction that only Scripture, not some particular interpretive schema, is transcultural. For the authority of Scripture reflects God's own transcendent authority over all cultures. And it is through Scripture—as this is read, taught, or preached—that God's presence is manifest in a given culture and people. What Indian evangelical theologian Samuel Sumithra says of Hindu culture could be applied more generally: "The primary issue here . . . is not the understanding of Christ in context, nor the Gospel in context. Evangelical theology is primarily the interpretation of the Bible in context" (in Ro and Eshenaur, 1984:220).

It might be thought that the bipolar character of the interaction tends to underplay the authority of Scripture, and for this reason some have preferrred to call it a hermeneutical spiral. But it is my contention that the authority of Scripture, though it is theoretically assumed at the beginning, must work itself out in actual practice. The authority, though it is accepted by faith, will be demonstrated in the actual transformation of life and thought that takes place by the ministry of the Holy Spirit. The important fact is not a theoretical authority but an actual authority in the life and thinking of the believer that reflects a living encounter with God. And this actual (practical) authority will emerge only from a serious interaction between Scripture and cultural realities. The truth of Scripture has to be worked down into the fabric of our lived worlds, and this takes place only through struggle and interaction with the actual problems of life.

It might also be thought that this dialogue downplays the role of the history and traditions of the church universal. But this is not the case. For the logical consequent of recognizing that both the life and teaching of the missionary/evangelist affect the interactional process is that these will eventually be understood in their historical (as well as their cultural) context. As these traditions interact with local traditions, an important role for the history of the church will emerge— though this history itself may be read in a new way.

What would be the implications of this model for the challenge facing Venkayya? I would argue that more important than the actual decision of whether to contribute to the sacrifice would be the process that would take place in Venkayya's Christian life—and in the village—as a result of this encounter. Let us consider first what might happen if he refuses to contribute to the sacrifice. It is possible that he would refuse to contribute and his daughter would still die. Then he would be forced to deal with the reality of tragedy and the seeming injustice of life (issues that Asian theologies often raise). Scripture would be heard in the light of these issues, and the cross and trials of Christians would take on new meaning and would in turn challenge the fatalism with which his neighbors would face the death of a child. The story of Scripture would show that life brings sorrow because of the brokenness and fallenness of the world. And it is just this world that God himself entered and suffered to restore.

But it must be acknowledged that making the hard decision to resist the pressure of the community will not in itself solve the problem of how this faith will work itself out in this particular community. Indeed, it is to leave this problem for another day, for it suggests that the Christian lives in some sense in opposition to his culture. But this question must still be faced: How will Christians come to terms with a village life permeated with curses and the need for sacrifices?

On the other hand, Venkayya may give in to the pressure and make a contribution. He may decide that expressing solidarity with his neighbors is more important than his convictions at this point—that the sacrifice is as much an expression of social solidarity as of religious ceremony. But this decision will surely send him back to Scripture (or to his missionary teacher) with a fresh determination to test these decisions. It may bring Christians from other villages to rally around in a new way that would itself be an argument for the truth of the Gospel. This decision inevitably commits him to working out his faith from within his culture, and it carries its own particular problems, calling perhaps for a greater correction from Scripture. But this may not be apparent to Venkayya at once.

In other words, this single decision Venkayya is called on to make, important as it is, must not be isolated from the larger context of what God wishes to see happen in Venkayya and his village. In a sense, facing this one challenge in isolation from what went before and what follows is easier than beginning a process in which the Word of God is allowed to take root and flourish in that family and that community.

These may seem like long thoughts for a simple villager in India, Africa, or Latin America. But it is precisely the challenges that face believers like Venkayya that make up the warp and woof of theology in the Third World. Although this story may seem simple and uncomplicated, all the issues of the Gospel and culture are implicated in the decision Venkayya is forced to make—tensions between community allegiance and commitment to God, the relation between God's power and other powers. Although he may not reflect on it until later (or ever!), the fact remains that God wants for him a development that moves him toward maturity in Christ—a growing wisdom and serenity in the values of the Gospel. And what he wants for that community is a fellowship of believers that confronts the worldview of that place with a perspective of hope in the God who raised Jesus from the dead. This will happen only if a serious interaction takes place between Scripture and the demands not only for sacrifice to the gods but also for backbreaking labor under the sun, with poor harvests and good, and with of all the dangers, toils, and snares of life in that particular place.

Whether we are somewhere near the mark will not appear until we have covered a great deal more ground and confronted many more issues. What we will watch for is whether the theology in question puts its weight down on Scripture or on culture as a primary reference point. Meanwhile we will let this stand as a hypothesis for one way in which Scripture may be related to culture—a hypothesis that our discussion in what follows may be allowed to test.

2

AFRICAN THEOLOGY: CHRISTIANITY AND CULTURE

The Story is everlasting . . . like Fire, when it is not blazing it is smouldering under its own ashes or sleeping and resting inside its flinthouse. When we are young and without experience we all imagine that the story of the land is easy, that everyone of us can get up and tell it. But that is not so. True we all have our scraps of tale bubbling in us. But what we tell is like the middle of a mighty boa which a foolish forester mistakes for a tree trunk and settles upon to take his snuff. (Chinua Achebe, Anthills of the Savannah. 1987:126)

THE AGENDA OF AFRICAN THEOLOGY

In Sierra Leone a family visits a cemetery to tell the ancestors about the impending marriage: Is everything in order? Are the prospects propitious? They pour drink on the ground and scatter cola nuts. If the cola nuts land in the proper way, all will go well; if the nuts do not land as desired, they are thrown again. In this way for generations Africans have played out their fears and faith at every crisis point—of marriage, childbirth, and illness, of crops, rains and harvests. And it is in just such a setting—this-worldly, yet faith-filled— that Christianity has confronted Africans. "Because traditional religions permeate all departments of life," John Mbiti observes, "there is no formal distinction between the sacred and the secular . . . between the spiritual and material areas of life" (1969:2). So every area of life raises religious questions. How will the Gospel take shape in this setting? The Seoul Declara-

35

tion of Evangelical Third World theologians concluded that African theology will have to "take seriously the traditional African worldview, the reality of the spirit world, [and] the competing ideologies" (1983:11).

Reference to competing ideologies reminds us that there is a black liberation theology which has been influential in Africa, especially in the south. But outside South Africa this is clearly not a dominant interest (though Gwinyai Muzorewa, writing in Zimbabwe, wishes it were [1984:55]). John Mbiti has argued in several places that African theology begins more often with a shout of joy and with an affirmation of life than with a cry for deliverance (see the discussion in Onwu 1986:32–33). Theologians, then, as Muzorewa says, "have focused on Africanization" (1984:55).

The need to root faith in one's setting and in one's history: this great theme provides African theology with its great opportunity, and, we will note, its biggest challenge. It is hard to overstate the need for this in a fragmented modern world on the verge of losing its soul as it rushes into the future. We will argue that it may be Africa's role to help us see life as a single reality in which both material and spiritual dimensions have a place. As a recent conference of the Fraternity of Evangelical Theologians in Africa noted, "In Africa, perhaps as nowhere else, the holistic approach is distinctive" (Gitari and Benson, 1986:vii).

But first it is important to discover what gives African theology this particular agenda: Why have theologians been so concerned with these particular questions?

HISTORICAL SETTING OF AFRICAN THEOLOGY

One could argue that the problem of theology in Africa has been highlighted by the very success of Christianity in that region. The facts are by now familiar to almost everyone. Since 1900, Christians have increased in Africa by a factor of 25 and are now more numerous than those in North America. Between 1980 and 1988 alone, Christians in Africa have grown from 164 million to 212 million; this works out to more than 16,000 new Christians every day! (David Barrett's figures are conveniently summarized in Mbiti, 1986:235–41; see also Barrett, 1988).

Since the Christian population in parts of Africa may now be anywhere between 40 and 90 percent of the population, the question of the relation of this new thing in Africa to her history and her traditions becomes urgent: Is there really an African Christianity? And what shape should it take?

The dilemma is posed by two conflicting realities within the African church: the persistent (and growing) influence of traditional religious beliefs and the uncompromising teaching of the missionary leaders that these things are part of the world of sin and darkness that must be repudiated. This tension, and the anguish and misunderstanding it has caused to both parties, must be the starting point for any discussion of theology in Africa.

Let us begin with the second issue. No colonized Third World country has been quick to praise her former rulers, but in no part of the world is the feeling stronger than in Africa that colonialism has left a permanent scar on the soul of the people. In Latin America it is the economic oppression that resulted from colonialism and neocolonialism that is the object of attack; in Africa it is the cultural damage that is remembered.

The history of missions in Africa seems dominated by strong individuals, individuals who sometimes combined incredible strength of character with an insensitivity to local traditions. Robert Moffat (1795–1883), for example, is remembered for his outstanding work of evangelism and Bible translation in Kuruman, southern Africa. But Stephen Neill is forced to conclude:

> In spite of his love for the Africans, he had little interest in the background of their thought. . . . He underestimated their religious traditions, and introduced the fervent Evangelical Christianity of his own tradition, without considering the possibilities of its adaptation to an African world. (1947:313)

David Livingstone (1818–1873) went to Africa in 1841 both to convert people to Christianity and to put an end to the slave trade. But he knew that stopping slavery would not solve the continent's problems unless new systems of commerce were introduced. For Livingstone these could only be European. Following his tireless explorations throughout south central Africa, he returned to England in 1857 to make a final appeal for support in opening Africa. In a famous speech at Cambridge he pleaded:

> I beg to direct your attention to Africa. I know that in a few years I shall be cut off in that country, which is now open. Do not let it be shut again! I go back to Africa to try to make an open path for commerce and Christianity. *Do you carry on the work which I have begun? I leave it with you.* (ibid., 315, his emphasis)

Although, like many others of his century, he was clearly motivated by the kingdom of Christ, this kingdom brought with it much "indirect fruit" that looked suspiciously like European civilization.

In 1885 at the Berlin Conference the dominant European powers divided up the continent of Africa according to maps that were wildly inaccurate and by principles obscure to all but the participants. The "darkness" of Africa may have had something to do with the European angle of vision! Although Christianity was not specifically named in these treaties, religious missions were given special privileges that were to have important consequences (see the discussion of this period in Dickson, 1984: chapter 3).

Although missionaries introduced principles that were later to have great importance in African independence movements and although they often championed native rights, they were inevitably influenced by the extreme ethnocentrism of Western culture. Jon Bonk in his study of missionary attitudes points out that as late as 1916 no one in the West doubted the superiority of the white race. He notes with tongue in cheek: "Missionaries could not be expected to match in scientific sophistication the racist-imperialist thinking of the leading intellectuals of the time, but they could hardly have been unaffected by it" (1980:299).

There could be no question then, for the early missionaries, that to become a Christian in Africa meant to give up completely the "pagan" ways of the ancestors and take on the Christian ways of the West. What Bolaji Idowu says of Nigeria could apply to many other places in Africa:

> If at the beginning, anyone had had enough vision to suggest that while accepting Christianity, Nigerians did not need to throw away what was good and valuable in their own culture, such a person would have been accused of rank "heathenism" by the European religious educators whose set purpose was to exterminate as of the Devil anything that had no meaning for them. (1965:5)

This situation has been aggravated, since the war, by the second reality: the resurgence of African religious traditions. Accompanying the independence movements of the 1950s was an attempt to recover links with an African past. *Uhuru,* freedom, meant also the freedom to be African. African religions became the object of sustained and highly sophisticated study. E. G. Parrinder's ground-breaking study *African Traditional Religion* was published in 1954, E. E. Evans-Pritchard's classic study *Nuer Religion* appeared in 1956, and E. Bolaji Idowu's text followed in 1973. In the latter, Idowu defines the resurgence in the following way:

> The eyes of African peoples, especially African scholars, are being opened to the fact that they have a certain God-given heritage which has its own intrinsic values with which is bound the destiny of their racial soul. These values they are seeking to recover or refurbish. (1973:x)

The fact that Idowu is a committed Christian only makes his position all the more poignant: What is a Christian committed to the Gospel to make of the traditions he has been taught to denigrate? In an important article Nlenanya Onwu summarizes the sentiments of many others: "Post-missionary Christianity in Africa with its links with colonialism, capitalism and its abstract proclamation of the gospel has created cultural confusion, and a deep spiritual crisis in the African society today" (1986:37).

That this crisis reaches to the "hankering depths of Africa's soul" (Onwu's expression) is obvious to anyone exposed to African literature. Almost everything written deals in some way or other with the missionaries; many of the best novels focus on the poignant dilemma of bright forward-looking young people caught between the missionaries' vision of life and the ways of the fathers. Kenyan Ngugi wa Thiong'o's book *The River Between* literally places the village and the church on opposite ridges, and the hero Waiyaki is forced to choose between them. In Nigerian Chinua Achebe's classic *Things Fall Apart* this conflict is presented as the undoing of Africa. There an elder is asked if the missionary understands their ways. He answers:

> How can he when he does not even speak our tongue? But he says our customs are bad; and our brothers who have taken up his religion also say that our customs are bad. How do you think we can fight when our own brothers have turned against us? The white man is very clever. He came quietly and peaceably with his religion. We were amused at his foolishness and allowed him to stay. Now he has won our brothers, and our clan can no longer act like one. He has put a knife on the things that held us together and we have fallen apart. (1958:124–25)

It is not surprising, then, that this crisis provides the central problem for African theology today. Ghanaian Kwame Bediako in his 1983 thesis lays out the issues most clearly. It is not simply a matter of a European ethnocentrism that left a lingering sense of cultural inferiority, though this is bad enough. The problem for Christians turned out to be a deeper, theological one. For "theological consciousness presupposes a religious tradition, and tradition requires memory, and memory is integral to identity" (1983:294). But this kind of memory was denied African Christians. They were asked to repudiate their past and live off a borrowed heritage. Finding their identity, then, as Christians will surely involve the exploration and reconstitution of their "roots." This challenge gives theology in Africa its particular excitement and its special perils.

Ample evidence for this is given by the phenomenal growth of the African Independent Churches (see Barrett, 1968). Numbering now between 10 and 20 million, these groups have arisen under strong indigenous leaders who have dared make use of local traditions. Whereas missionary churches are sometimes skeptical about the reality of spiritual powers that people the African imagination, "it is often only the independent churches that show genuine awareness and concern about them—through prayer, exorcism, ritual, anointing, fasting, use of Bible verses and ablutions" (Mbiti, 1986:76; see also van Essen, 1977). Just as the Base Communities of Latin America give expression to their own spiritual and political needs, so these rapidly growing sects in Africa give expression to deeply felt spiritual and cultural values.

Ideally a study of African theology would make much use of the theology of these independent movements. But we are not yet in a position to assess their contribution adequately. This is partly because traditional theological method has not been able to deal with their eclectic and ad hoc character. Harry Sawyerr, following a study of the West African Aladura Church, reflected on this difficulty: "Flaws in the religious life of the Aladura make it unlikely that the advocates of African Theology can truly use the independent churches as their yardstick" (in Parratt, ed., 1987:20). There is, however, a growing anthropological literature on these groups that shows promise of contributing greatly to theological discussion in Africa. Bennetta Jules-Rosette, for example, conducted a thorough study of the Apostles of John Maranke (of south central Africa) and concluded that "Christianity provided the grammar and syntax and traditional customs the lexicon for the symbolic combination in Apostolic reasoning and ritual" (1975:190). Unfortunately theologians are only beginning to make use of these studies, and so our study will not include extended reference to these groups.

WHAT IS THE AFRICAN WORLDVIEW?

We turn now to a survey of the African worldview, which has received much attention in recent years. But at the outset we are faced with the issue of *which* African worldview to consider, for black (or Subsaharan) Africa, which is our major concern, consists of literally thousands of ethnic groups and subgroups. This problem, however, may be more apparent than real. Professor Idowu, in fact, has insisted, "It is not infrequently that foreign investigators over-emphasize or exaggerate the elements of variation and therefore fail to see the basic unity [among these groups]" (in Dickson and Ellingworth, 1969:11).

Early on, E. G. Parrinder argued that "the resemblances are far more important than the differences" (1974:11; first ed., 1954). That is, within the incredible variety of cultures and practices, general similarities can be noticed. This view has been confirmed by a recent study on the nature of African culture. Professor A. Ekweunife has argued that African culture possesses a unity in diversity. Within the larger world arc of cultural practices "Africa has her own pattern quite different from either European or American. . .patterns" (1987:16). So it seems safe to say that the variety of African cultures south of the Sahara form a single continuum of views that are distinctive to this continent and that can provide material for theological reflection that is African. Of course, doing theology in Africa will necessarily involve interaction with particular cultures. But our purpose is to learn from the general situation in Africa, and so I will emphasize the common elements. However, to avoid improper generalization, I will, wherever possible, refer to the actual source of practices and beliefs. The interested reader can then pursue more detailed descriptions by consulting the authorities listed in the notes.

BASIC ELEMENTS OF AN AFRICAN WORLDVIEW

Harmony

The Igbo of Nigeria have a word, *omenala*, that is best translated "decorum," and reflects an important character of African thought. The world and life are believed by many African peoples to reflect a fundamental harmony that religion and ritual are meant to preserve or enhance. The order seems to be fundamentally positive, and yet it is precarious and appears threatened from various directions.

The "harmony" may be preserved or even enhanced, but it preexists our efforts—the human community does not create it; it is given by God and the ancestors. And it is enshrined in the normal orders of life and death, rainy season and dry, planting and harvest. For the Mbuti (a Pygmy people of central Africa) "taboos and morning fire ceremony intimate that forest depths [where the people live] and humanity can be brought together in a greater harmony that preserves all things" (Zuesse, 1979:36). This account of an Epulu elder (from Zaire) graphically portrays this confidence in life:

> Normally everything goes well in our world. But at night when we are sleeping sometimes things go wrong, because we are not awake to stop them from going wrong. Army ants invade the camp; leopards may come in and steal a hunting dog or even a child. If we were awake these things would not happen. So when something big goes wrong, like illness or bad hunting or death, it must be because the forest is sleeping and not looking after its children. So what do we do? We wake it up by singing to it, and we do this because we want it to awaken happy. Then everything will be well and good again. So when our world is going well then also we sing to the forest because we want it to share our happiness. (In Zuesse, 43–44)

This description shows the ambivalence of the world. It is meant to go well, and it usually does. So in the morning prayer of an Abaluyia old man, God is addressed:

> O God, give me mercy upon our children who are suffering.
> Bring riches today as the sun rises;
> Bring all fortunes to me today. (Mbiti, 1969:62).

Or this Igbo morning prayer:

> Give us life,
> Worthwhile life. (Okorocha in Gitari and Benson, 199)

Nigerian scholar Cyril Okorocha argues, as we will note below, that it is precisely this hunger for worthwhile life that may serve as an entrance point for God's promise of abundant life in Christ.

But the darker side of life, its vulnerability, is equally important for theology. If life ordinarily goes well, it can also be threatened; indeed, at times life in Africa seems to be a constant struggle to fend off evil influences. For the traditional worldview, all change is viewed as a threat (Zuesse, 111) and problems are seen as analogous to death (Okorocha, in Gitari and Benson, 200). So rituals and prayers are meant to restore stability, as this Nandi ceremonial prayer (from Kenya) indicates:

> God, guard for me the children and cattle,
> God, guard for us the cattle,
> God, give us health! (Mbiti, 1975:60–61)

God and the Powers

For people in Africa the universe is alive and controlled by powers that sustain the harmony of everyday life. For some, the material world is a mirror of the spiritual world (Ogbu Kalu in Appiah-Kubi and Torres, 1979:15; see also Zuesse, 128). John Mbiti stresses the interconnection of these two worlds (1971:134–39). In any case the material and spiritual worlds are ultimately part of a single reality, and the line between the one and the other is difficult to draw.

But for all Africans the belief in a single, all-powerful *God* is unquestioned. In John Mbiti's study of over three hundred peoples in Africa, all had some notion of God as the supreme being (1969:29). In contrast to the West, most Africans believe in God as an unquestioned reality, the unique creator and controller of the universe. But exactly how God is related to the affairs of life is not altogether clear. Certain myths portray God as once living close to people, but, at some point, having withdrawn. The Ashanti of Ghana tell this story:

> A long, long time ago God lived close to people, hovering nearby, watching. One woman who was vigorously preparing the evening meal of fufu with her mortar and pestle struck against God with the long pestle and angered him. So God left his intimacy with people and went into the heavens. The communion of the golden age was broken. Now God is distant, but still rumbling in the thunder and spitting out the rain. (in Rubingh, 1974:3)

The Igbo of Nigeria speak of the time when God became tired of being bothered by every little complaint—a lost broom, a broken hoe, a domestic claim—and withdrew far above the heavens to do other things (Metuh, 1981:13). Emefie Metuh claims, however, that the thesis that God in Africa is distant and withdrawn is oversimplified: "The withdrawal of God as referred to in the myths must not be taken too literally. They only try to explain the universal human experience of divine transcendence." (ibid., 14)

Evidence for God's continuing presence lies in the fact that he may be appealed to directly in prayer. John Mbiti summarizes his study of African prayers by saying, "At least 90 per cent of the prayers are addressed to God. Therefore he emerges as the clearest and most concrete spiritual reality" (1975:4). This data, however, must be balanced by the fact that most sacrifices and ritual acts are not made with reference to God but to some lesser spirit or power. For there seems to be a reticence to approach God directly; African believers seem more comfortable appealing to some lesser power (though Charles Nyamiti may be going too far in characterizing the general attitude toward God as a practical atheism [in Parratt, ed., 1987:21]). At least God's distance is generally respected. The Fang (Gabon Pygmies) have this prayer:

Nzame [God] is on high, man below.
God is God, man is man,
Each is at home, each in his own house. (Zuesse, 1979:55)

Living in a close relation to God are the *spirits*. Called by various names, these are separate sources of power, created by God to mediate his power. The precise relation between God and the exercise of his power has been the subject of much debate (cf Metuh, 1981). Clearly these lesser spirits can be approached directly as ends in themselves; at the same time they cannot be regarded as independent deities—they share and mediate the power that properly belongs to God. So it seems safer to call African religion monotheistic—Idowu calls it a "diffused montheism" (1973:135)—rather than polytheistic, as has been the practice in the past. God is the source of power; the lesser beings are what might be called refractions of his power. Noel King calls the Orisa, the lesser divinities of the highly developed pantheon of the Yoruba people of Nigeria, "emanations of God's power" (1986:9).

What is significant is that the lesser divinities are intimately related to the particular situation and place of the people; they are called by special names and referred to as "our gods," and these gods are assigned particular roles in God's monarchial government (Idowu, 1973:170). All of this is not unlike the polytheism of Israel's neighbors in the Old Testament.

Sometimes distinguished from these divinities (especially in West Africa) are less clearly defined spirits. These are sometimes abstract powers that may take on various forms (as trees or rocks). Such spirits are often intimately associated with the weather or natural phenomena, which has for Africans religious significance. Nature in fact is often thought of as an imprint of the divine—God gives rain, speaks in the thunder, walks in the earthquake (Mbiti, 1969:41–48, 76–77).

The nature of what are called evil spirits is difficult to define and reveals the same ambivalence that we saw in relation to God himself. Spirits in general are regarded with dread, though they can be bargained with or controlled by magic. In some religious systems—notably the Esha spirits of the Yoruba—there are particular evil spirits. For the most part, however, spirits causing trouble are not a separate class of beings so much as ordinary spirits who have become angry for one reason or another. The nature and origin of evil will occupy us in some detail below, but for now it is enough to remind ourselves that for Africans all evil events are "caused" by some spiritual power. It seems ordinarily that these result from the violation of some taboo or some ritual omission (in other words, the source of the evil is here on earth). But Africans have expressed to me that they sometimes feel that people are made to suffer because of some quarrel or conflict that exists in the world of the powers (that is, evil can have its source in the spiritual realm). The diversity of these views, and their possible reconciliation, will be of great significance for an African reading of Scripture.

Closer to the living community, though still in the spiritual realm, are the *ancestors* who have recently died and are sometimes called the living or lively dead. It is hard to overemphasize the importance of ancestors for the African worldview. Since the spirit world is so close, departure to that world (the common understanding of death) is a central event in the life of the community (Mbiti found twenty-five different words for it in Akamba, 1971:129). It seems that primarily those who have been elders and had stature in the community can become "ancestors." As they have represented the stability of the community in life, after death they remain a vital part of the community. S. N. Ezeanya goes so far as to say, "Life from day to day—we might legitimately say from moment to moment—has no meaning at all apart from the ancestral presence and power" (in Dickson and Ellingworth, 1969:43).

The ancestors mediate power, but Kwame Bediako dislikes reference to a hierarchy, because the living dead are often appealed to as ends in themselves (in Gitari and Benson, 92). For the Shona they are perfectly purged of all evil (Muzorewa, 1984:13–14). For many others they are the custodians of the morality of the people. The same ambiguity that we have noticed previously pervades feelings toward the ancestors.

They must be acknowledged as close and important, though they must be "managed" by proper ritual acts and sacrifices (Mbiti, 1971:134). Their presence is acknowledged and even appreciated and yet it is also feared.

Parrinder reports that in Ghana the people are not nearly as afraid of their gods as they are of their ancestors (1974:59). Ancestors may be the cause of any evil that happens: drought, famine, even sickness and death. But they may also be the source of fertility, both of crops and of the womb. All of this points up the fact that the ancestors' relation to the living world is closer than either the divinities or God himself, and thus they are seen as mediators of the powers coming ultimately from God.

The ancestors remain important until enough time has elapsed for them to pass out of living memory and finally disintegrate into the corporate memory of the tribe (Mbiti, 1971:139. Mbiti is describing his own Akamba people of Kenya; his term for this is "mechanical immortality"). Meanwhile no significant event takes place without some reference to the continuing presence of these living dead.

Finally, no discussion of the powers would be complete without some reference to the *human mediators* of this power on earth. Consistent with the view that God (or even the gods) must not be approached directly, Africans feel that one should seek the mediation of specialists. The most common of these are the priests, who, especially in West Africa, are highly trained and sometimes attached to temples where offerings are brought. Chiefs, elders, or fathers, as representatives of the people, both living and dead, may be called on to offer sacrifices.

Associated with the priests are the mediums, who are "possessed" with the spirit of a god or ancestor and give messages from this realm. Diviners, on the other hand, are called on to diagnose an illness or problem and prescribe an appropriate remedy. Medicine men (often called herbalists today) are those with the widest knowledge both of natural remedies and of spiritual powers. John Mbiti reports that many well-educated herbalists are known to work side by side with doctors in Africa today (see Parrinder, 1974:100–109, and Mbiti, 1971:69, 166–73).

All of these human mediators perform rituals necessary to the proper ordering of life. And to Africans, contrary to the impression conveyed sometimes in Western literature, they ordinarily play a positive role in society, promoting the general harmony. But it seems, according to R. B. Kitongi, that they are best considered mediators between the human world and the spirit world in general, rather than between God and humans (in Dickson and Ellingworth, 54). This is consistent with Mbiti's observation that prophets, as those who speak from God and announce the future, do not exist in African traditional societies (1971:190). Again the connection between God and this world is ordinarily indirect, for the power sought is for maintaining the order of the human community, as it is, and not to introduce God's special purposes onto the human plane. The significance of this for Christian reflection will be considered further on.

The Human Community

It is safe to say that the whole living, pulsating universe comes to focus on the human community. Harry Sawyerr comments, "The worship of ancestors, the attitude to birth, death, sin, sickness, forgiveness and health converge on the central role of the community" (in Parratt, 1987:23).

The human person plays a central role in all African thinking, but always in the context of the community. Among the Epulu, a forest people, the person is said to dwell in the midst of divine fullness that is reflected in the pepo, "soul" or "life force." This pepo animates all living beings and the human pepo participates in and condenses this fullness (Zuesse, 1979:18). Among the Igbo each person is endowed with his own personal chi by the almighty Chi and so is sacrosanct. To live is to participate in the life of the spiritual world (Okorocha, 1987:78). So the person cannot be destroyed, his or her existence is tied to the unity of all that exists. As Mbiti describes it, this is an intensely anthropocentric ontology. It is a unity centered on humanity, in such a way that death cannot destroy it. To destroy humanity would, in effect, mean destroying the whole coherence of being, including the Creator (1971:132).

But this human centeredness is a social and communitarian notion. A person's success, identity, and well-being are all dependent on being in tune with one's community. An argument between husband and wife is an affair not only of that household but also of the whole village. For it destroys the coherence that holds things together. Many of the cultural practices—e.g., initiation rites, age grade systems, secret societies—are meant to affirm and sustain this community and the identity of individuals within it (see Kalu in Appiah-Kubi; Torres, 1979:17; and Zuesse, 1979:65).

Positively, the community is to manifest itself in a life of sharing. Traditionally, in many groups land has been communally held. Today this fundamental value has influenced political life throughout Africa, from *ujamaa* (Tanzanian socialism) to the one-party system. The strengths of these values are obvious to anyone who has experienced the social and psychic isolation of Western individualism, but the dangers should be recognized as well. As K. Bediako points out, the weakness of African thinking is reflected in a tendency to sacralize the human (in Gitari and Benson, 1986:88). This is illustrated in Evan Zuesse's description of the Ila people of Zambia:

> Even the emphasis on the role-relationships that control our ritual cooperation raises us from the merely egoistical to the transcendental level, since we enter these roles to sustain an order beyond ourselves. We submit finally not to a social order but to a cosmic community of spirits and norms, anchored in mysterious power. (1979:86)

Means of Fellowship

We have noticed how intrinsic religious life is to the African. The nature of this religious attitude, however, needs careful definition. In an interesting article Ghanian J. N.

Kudadjie takes on the view that all of life in Africa is determined by religious interest, and he concludes that social sanctions are as important in Africa as religious ones (see J. S. Pobee, ed., 1976:60–77). But such discussion may rest on a failure to recognize the unique character of religion in Africa. As John Mbiti—who is a particular object of Kudadjie's attack—points out, religion in Africa is "utilitarian, not purely spiritual, it is practical not mystical" (1969:67). That is to say, the object of ritual and cultic acts is to sustain the social and the cosmic order—the two can hardly be separated.

So the means of fellowship are not meant to provide for communion with the gods but to enlist these powers in support of the community. The diviner we noted is to discover the cause of a misfortune and counteract this influence by an appropriate ritual. Nigerian Cyril Okorocha summarizes:

> The world around [the African] is peopled by a whole universe of beings and therefore his whole religious effort is to find the way or means whereby he can manipulate to his own advantage through prayer and ritual, the powers inherent in the "spirit forces." (1987:52)

Rituals are primarily of two kinds: sacrifices and magic. Sacrifices and libations are meant to appeal to the goodwill of the gods or spirits; magic (both white and black) seeks to manipulate in more mechanical ways forces that cannot be dealt with by appeal. Magic deals with spiritual forces, however, even if they are "lower" on the hierarchy of forces. In sacrifices and libations the gift element is primary, one gives in order to curry favor in return. The assumption is that these powers—usually the lesser spirits or ancestors—are susceptible to this kind of human appeal (on this see Sawyerr in Dickson and Ellingworth, 1969:64, 74, 49, and Parrinder, 1974:113–14).

These acts all seek to preserve the social order, but it is clear by now that this order is never conceived in isolation from the world of God. To the Dinkas of Sudan sacrifices are the perpetual link between the plane of people and that of God (Mbiti, 1969:61). Even initiation rites are a protest against the disintegration of the community and an affirmation of unity with a more enduring order. Evan Zuesse characterizes sacrifices without too much exaggeration as an offering of one's existence to the divine order so as to receive it back conformed to the divine order (1979:216). In any reflection on this worldview key questions emerge: Is the primordial order actually creative? Is it able to intervene in any way that can transform this human order? Or is the human order finally determinative of human needs and destiny? These are some of the questions that African cultures pose to the Christian Scriptures. To the interaction between these two we now turn.

THEOLOGICAL PERSPECTIVES

Some such framework, however altered by education and travel, is formative for most Africans even today–though exactly to what extent this is true we will want to explore later. In any case, for African theologians who feel they have been systematically deprived of their heritage, serious reflection on this worldview has become an important starting point. But granted the importance of this background of thought, the constructive work remains to be done: How will this context influence the shape of theology done in this region? Although the discussion is only beginning, there are indications of the directions it will take. We consider three areas here as examples: the quest for life, evil, and deliverance; God and the Spirits; and time and history (leaving a discussion on Christology to a later chapter).

The Quest for Life, Evil, and Deliverance

To say that African religion has a utilitarian character, as John Mbiti has done, without clarification, is to risk misunderstanding. Africans do seek crops, health, and children, not necessarily as ends in themselves, but as means to a particular kind of life. Cyril Okorocha has stressed in his book on salvation that the Igbo of Nigeria seek not just to live, but to live a viable or fulfilled life (what they call *ezi-ndu*). "To the

Igbo, no religious experience is deemed sufficient that does not lead to the emergence of life and the enlargement of it so that it becomes viable" (1987:69).

This conforms with our observation that, for the African, the order of life has a positive character to it. And it echoes Mbiti's insistence that African theology begins more with a shout of joy than a cry for deliverance. Life for Africans is to be lived celebrationally. So religion seeks to embody a positive response to life that is instinctive and elemental, one that is swept along by the energies of the universe.

In traditional religion, the intricate system of taboos and rituals are designed to protect the integrity of this order, so that life can be affirmed. In the religion of the Nuer (of Sudan) E. E. Evans-Pritchard has described the elaborate meaning associated with the word *thek*. The basic meaning is to "respect"; it calls on the person concerned to avoid or abstain from the object or act in question. These values, he says, "are intended to keep people apart from other people or from creatures or things" (1956:181). To violate this order is shameful and leaves the person (and even those near him or her) polluted or even sick, and it entails religious sanctions. These restrictions (and indeed most taboos) arise out of the basic social order and are intended to preserve that order. If they are violated, it is believed that God himself will punish the offender (ibid., 189).

It is interesting that the Nuer do not generally blame the person in the wrong; indeed mistakes are often inadvertent. But "the man who commits them. . .places himself, and possibly others too, in danger of having done something that brings Spirit into action in the affairs of men" (ibid., 190). So what makes an action bad is not its intrinsic character, but the bad consequences it brings on the community; and what is at stake with the individuals committing the "sin" is not their morals, but the resultant spiritual condition: they become polluted or unclean. As a result some sacrifice is called for to remedy the situation (ibid., 195).

Against this background, sin is not primarily understood as an individual affair, but rather as a social reality. Metuh generalizes from his study of African morality that offenses are all "disruptions of the harmonious relationship in the ontological order" (1981:109), and they must be dealt with if the community is to survive. There is some parallel here to the teaching of Paul in Romans, especially chapter 5. There it is clear that sin has infected the whole of society through the sin of one man, Adam. "As sin entered the world through one man, and death through sin, and in this way death came to all men, because all sinned . . ." (Rom. 5:12). This conception, that the race has been polluted by the sin of Adam, so offensive to the individualism of the West, seems perfectly comprehensible to an African. Notice too that the African teaching (like Paul's) seems to be that we sin because we are sinners, that is, polluted, and not the reverse. It is the spiritual condition of the person that is the problem and not simply the acts performed.

Reference to this biblical passage raises the question as to whether there is, in the African view, an original event like the sin of Adam that has left its mark on human society. The answer is that the myths of Africa contain interesting echoes of such an event. According to one Igbo myth, there was no evil in the beginning. Whenever people needed anything, they sent to Chukwu (God), and he would send it to them. Once he sent the vulture, which was then a beautiful bird, to deliver a big parcel to mankind, with careful instructions not to open it on the way. The vulture disobeyed God, and when he opened the package, all kinds of evil were poured out on the earth. This is why to this day the vulture is always eating dead things and garbage, trying vainly to clean up the mess he has made on the earth (Metuh, 1981:15).

This story illumines the presence of evil in the world in a way that recalls the Genesis account. The earth was once good, but something "happened" to upset this harmony. This event was not God's doing, though he was necessarily involved in its consequences. But there seems to be no consciousness of how this original event, though clearly the cause of evil in the world, is related to individual violations of taboos. Here the biblical story (and its commentary in Romans 5) makes an explicit connection: we sin because of the pollution caused by the original evil event. The Bible then deepens the understanding of evil by insisting that the original "fall" has resulted in a general pollution that affects the whole world (Rom. 3:10–18). Moreover, this state calls forth the just response of God himself, which is expressed as our being under his wrath (1:18).

As a result of the dissociation of present sins from the original "mistake," deliverance from evil, in African religion, appears as a piecemeal or temporary solution. Although Africans have a sense that the world is abnormal, they cannot relate this abnormality to a general pollution resulting from the original "fall." And so each lapse calls for a fresh sacrificial intervention. John Mbiti concludes:

> Behind these fleeting glimpses of the original state and bliss of man, there lies the tantalizing and unattained gift of the resurrection, the loss of human immortality and the monster death. *Here*, African religions. . .must admit a defeat; they have supplied no solution. (1969:99, his emphasis; see the discussion in Adeyemo, 1979: 58, 59)

It is interesting that the Nuer people associate being in the right (i.e., not polluted) with "deliverance" (1956:27), implying that religion supplies power to change their spiritual situation. But again, where is power to be found that reverses the fundamental curse under which all people labor? Romans 5 contains an important parallel. Just as Adam's original sin brought about a general situation of pollution, so the New Adam, Christ, has brought about a righteous order. "If, by the trespass of the one man, death reigned through that one man, how much more will those who receive God's abundant provision of grace and of the gift of righteousness reign in life through the one man, Jesus Christ" (Rom. 5:17).

It would seem that the key is to see the problems of life— sickness, crop loss, even spells and curses so significant to Africans—as manifestations of the larger problem of sin and death in the world. The failure to make this connection represents the great weakness of African traditional faiths and an opportunity for Christianity.

In an interesting discussion of these issues, Maryknoll

missionary John Ganly recounts his struggle, while working with the Bakaonde of Zambia, to confront the problems of witchcraft among the people. He came to believe that the answer was not to deny the reality of this power, a route that missionaries had usually taken. In fact he believed that the key was to be found in the Kaonde version of the creation myth, which is an African version of Pandora's box, much like the Igbo myth recounted above. When he was subsequently confronted with a case of witchcraft in which a spell cast over a village was causing illness and death, he decided to address the issue in terms of the larger problem of "pollution" caused by the original disobedience.

Ganly gathered the whole village together to address them. Your myths tell you, he explained, that evil came into the world because of sin—he referred to their myth of the "fall." They all nodded their heads in agreement. "Now witchcraft is evil. Therefore, if we wish to remove evil, we must remove sin" (Ganly, 1985:349)—that is, we must somehow remove this original pollution. He then instructed the women of the village to come forward as representatives of the community (the Bakaonde are matrilineal) to confess their sins and lay them before the people. When they had done this, he told them: The evil of the village is here before us. Will you take this back to your houses or leave it here and follow God's way of life? If you follow God, the spell will be finished and life will begin.

There are aspects of Ganly's approach I have omitted—such as emphasizing Christ's death as the sacrifice for this sin. But notice how the emphasis on "life" recalls Okorocha's original point. Africans search for a full life, and the shape this search takes may provide one key to relating the Gospel to that context. Notice that Christianity claims not only to have provided, through Christ's death, a sacrifice to remedy the general pollution, but also to offer through his resurrection and the gift of the Holy Spirit spiritual power to achieve a new standard of living. Okorocha has shown how the Igbo believed that the coming of Christianity to Igboland brought what to their minds was a new age—education, hospitals, commerce.

"The search for education and a new way of attaining wealth was, to their minds, a search for salvation" (1987:234). This the old gods could not offer, and so there was a drift in the direction of power. But this power could be made available only when the previous issue of human pollution had been dealt with.

God and the Spirits

We have seen that most Africans believe that there is one who is creator and sustainer of all things. He is uniquely associated with the sky or the mountains, yet present at all times and places. In worship their deep sense of mystery and awe is pervasive. Is it true then, as Murorewa claims, that "African traditional religions provide African [Christian] theology with a theological framework in which the latter can develop" (1984:18)?

Ordinarily missionaries did identify the God of the Bible with the high god of African religions. But this identification, while initially appropriate (compare Paul's strategy in Acts 17), should have led to a new scrutiny of the biblical record in the light of the African worldview. In the New Testament it is clear that all power has come to focus on the authority of Christ (see Col. 1:15–20); this authority has been won by his victory on the cross (2:14–15). Moreover this divine authority is actively exercised in the world in pursuit of Christ's purposes of making disciples (Matt. 28:18–20).

In African religions, however, while there is a central authority, there is a diffused exercise of power. And it is not always clear what the relation is between the authority and the powers. Kwame Bediako notes, "The plurality of the primal world mirrors the primal apprehension of the divine as essentially pervasive, many faceted and ubiquitous" (article in Gitari and Benson, 1986:83, 85). The problem is that the plurality threatens the primary authority and lends an air of uncertainty to the operations of the spiritual world. "The plurality of divinities and spirit powers, with the concommitant multiplicity of worships and devotions, must ultimately weaken the human grasp of the unity of all things" (ibid., 87).

This leads to the tendency to give only conditional allegiance to any particular power—an allegiance that Okorocha refers to as reciprocal worship (see 1987:206). Although Africans are a people given to prayer at any time, they tend to worship God or gods for what they can get, not absolutely and unconditionally. When a greater power appears, Okorocha claims, they have no scruples about changing allegiance.

If this is so, coming to Christianity can be seen as liberation from the caprice of multiple powers. While the Bible does not deny the reality of these other powers, it places them clearly under the authority of the one God. So the believer is delivered from the fear of the uncertainty of the powers. The authority of God "excludes all notions of 'ancestral' mediation or veneration and other additions of 'spiritual forces' from a truly Christian account of the divine presence and working" (Bediako, in Gitari and Benson, 1986:91; see also the discussion in Tite Tienou, 1983:89−101).

The plenitude of powers in African religions appears, then, in Christianity to be concentrated in the divine fullness that is called the Trinity. As Charles Nyamiti notes, "If God is the life-giver, he is also the giver of power" (n.d. 54). This idea of the fullness of power and of life, so important to African beliefs, may, understood properly, throw fresh light on the biblical teaching on the divine life. The African seeks oneness through participation with the sources of life and power, through sharing. Could it be that the secret of God's power lies in the communication and sharing that takes place within the Godhead? Here the African understanding of participation may provide a fruitful model for enriching our understanding of the Trinity (which is often construed in a Western individualistic way; see ibid., 62−63).

But there is a further dimension to God's authority that is relevant to this discussion. In Scripture God exercises his authority by calling individuals (Abraham, Moses) and peoples (Israel, Judah) to serve him. In the New Testament Christ is revealed as the Lord to whom believers pray and who leads individual Christians in particular ways. We have seen that direct recourse to God is rare in African religions—recall Charles Nyamiti's accusation of practical atheism. And Harry Sawyerr claims, "So indeed whilst, like the Christian, African peoples for the most part believe in one supreme being, at the same time, he is not the principal directing agent of the historical factors of life" (in ibid., 21).

While we in the West may admire the unity and sharing practiced by traditional African societies, there is lacking a center and focus to this unity that recalls the Athenians' altar to the unknown God. Here the call of Christ comes to all those who are weary and burdened (Matt. 11:28)—especially those burdened by religious uncertainties. As J. V. Taylor writes of the impact of the Gospel in Africa: "This discovery that the vague distant creator is the centre and focus of every moment of all being is so catastrophic that it may overshadow for a time everything else in the Gospel" (1963:122).

The Meaning of Time and History

All of this raises the question of the meaning of time and history in Africa. In one sense the times of life and the movement of the seasons are central to the African consciousness. On the other hand, time lacks a future focus and so there is no sense that progress can be made toward any particular goal, no sense of what we in the West would call history.

At least this last view is the conclusion of the study of the concept of time in the Akamba culture of Kenya by John Mbiti. This study comprised Mbiti's 1963 doctoral dissertation at Cambridge and was published in 1971; it remains an important and pioneering study in cross-cultural theology. His argument is that time, for the Akamba, is a succession of events that move from the future into the past. "People look more to the 'past' for the orientation of their being than to anything that might yet come into human history" (1971:24–25). True, myths about the past give meaning to the future, but there are few myths that relate to particular future events.

Much of the evidence Mbiti adduces is linguistic. Verb tenses in Kikamba are present and past; people's concern focuses on the present (*mituki* is a highly dynamic present) and the recent past (*tene*). As a result there is no goal or climax imagined for history, in fact the "goal" of events, Mbiti insists, is in the past. People and events are swept away from the *mituki* to the *tene* and finally melt away in the unremembered past (ibid., 29). The argument that the Akamba (and by analogy many other African peoples) have no sense of the future has been the subject of severe criticism (the controversy is discussed with references in Gehman, 1987:64–71). It appears that many African languages (even, Gehman insists, Kikamba) do have an indefinite future, that is much the same as the indefinite past. Moreover, the very fact that African cultures treasure children and plan for their future indicates that they have a keen sense of the future.

But the point of Mbiti's argument seems to stand up to these criticisms: African cultures do not have a sense of crucial future events toward which things are moving and that influence the present. As Kwame Bediako points out in his defense of Mbiti's view, African ontology focuses on an "existential trajectory" that has as its goal the "preservation of the ancestral memory by the living community" (1983:396–99).

So the focus of life (and of traditional religion) is on the crisis points of life: birth, death, ancestral memory. 'Zulu Sofola elaborates these crises as the passage from the emergence of being from a "force," through its appearance on earth (birth), initiation into adulthood, death, and (in some cultures) transmigration or return to its source (in Appiah-Kofi and Torres, 1979:127–132). These events, seen by Sofola as the key to understanding African drama, have decisive influence on the "meaning of existence and the realization of its fulness" (ibid., 128).

Note that these crisis points are not only those events around which human life and the community are oriented, but they are also the point at which the spirit world is integrated into this world. In fact, one could go so far as to say that the meaning of the spirit world and its forces center on this trajectory of events. (Again, there are isolated instances where quarreling among the spirits appears to cause undeserved problems that must be dealt with by sacrifice, but there is no sense that events in that other world are crucial to the drama taking place here.) The earthly drama has absorbed all interest and meaning, it appears even to have drawn the life out of the spirit world.

But Mbiti's study is important also because it is one of the few places where a serious interaction with biblical material is attempted. For he points out that in the biblical view it is not human reality that provides coherence to reality, but Christ who has brought together the meaning of the world of God and our human world. "The incarnation brings the spirit world into the physical, so that the person who is in Christ is enabled to live simultaneously in both worlds" (1983:143). By participating in Christ's resurrection through baptism, the individual is rescued from *tene* into a vivid *mituki* of Christ's life—a permanent present involving the whole of creation. Here Mbiti elaborates Taylor's observation of the importance of Christ's work in centering time and history. P. E. S. Thompson points out the interesting fact that sacrifices in African traditional religion look forward to future benefits; the Christian looks backward to what has already been accomplished in the decisive correction on the cross (in Glasswell and Fashole-Luke, 1974:20).

But just at the point where the biblical material would make the most contribution to the African worldview—with its keen expectation of Christ's return and the revelation of his redemptive work—Mbiti hesitates. For he has been influenced by a particular interpretation of biblical eschatology (influenced in turn by Greek philosophy), in which the event of being in Christ is a timeless present—"impervious to temporal limitations" (1983:182. The influence of his Cambridge professors, C. H. Dodd and others, is clear, see 42–43). On this view of things, the appearing of Christ, then, is not so much an actual future event toward which history is moving, as an intensification of our present life in Christ. Historical and

materialistic references—e.g., his "coming in the clouds"—
are symbolic of what is otherwise beyond our understanding
(ibid., 89).

Some of Mbiti's views are clearly formed in reaction to the
teaching of the African Inland Church, in which he was raised.
That theology, in his mind, overemphasized the actual physical return of Christ to deliver his church from this evil world,
resulting in a spirituality that failed to give adequate importance to life in this world (ibid., 59–61). Yet he has to admit
that this teaching has found a ready response among his
people (at the time he wrote, a third of the one million Akamba
people had become Christians; the percentage is much higher
today). He also admits that the African Independent Churches
have flourished by focusing on this dimension of Christ's
work. It would appear that the hope of actual future deliverance seems to fulfill a deep-seated need in the African soul
(see Kato's discussion in 1975:77–88). The eager response in
fact may be part of the reason for the imbalance that Mbiti
pointed out: in evangelical churches in general (and not only
in Africa!) the present and future work of Christ is sometimes
not held together as it ought to be, and so it is not seen that
what Christ is already doing with his creation will be climaxed
and perfected when he comes again.

In a study of the Lord's Prayer Cyril Okorocha presents
what may be a better model of the interaction of Scripture and
African culture. Okorocha picks up on the present orientation
of African thought in a positive way. Africans desperately
want deliverance from the vulnerable life they lead now to a
life of fullness. This is what the return of Christ promises—
and this also explains why this belief is so precious to the
African Church. But for Africans, Okorocha insists, it is
difficult to look forward to a blessed hereafter unless there has
been a tangible "down payment" of that tomorrow in the here
and now. He sees this reflected in the phrase of the Lord's
Prayer "Give us already today, some of tomorrow's bread."
The concrete provision of needs now becomes, for children of
the heavenly Father, a symbol of the future that will be

completely manifest at Christ's return (in Gitari and Benson, eds., 1986:200).

Although we will return to this in our discussion of Christology in a later chapter, here we note how Christ's work on the cross and his return tie this world and its dramas together with the world of God and his purposes. It is in that larger story that the human drama with its greedy need and its joyous celebration, so important to the African, finds its real meaning.

CONCLUSION: TOWARD AN AFRICAN CHRISTIANITY ROOTED IN CULTURE

The crisis of human identity in the modern world has economic, educational, and political dimensions, but for Africans it is primarily a religious challenge. As a result, what is termed "progress" in the West is often viewed negatively in Africa. As John Mbiti put it, "The speed of casting off the scales of traditional life is much greater than the speed of wearing the garments of this future dimension of life" (1969:221). Secularism and industrialization are thus dehumanizing (ibid., 274), posing a problem that is ultimately religious.

This explains the eager search among traditional religious values, even on the part of Christian theologians, to find guidance, or at least a sense of balance, in the process of modernization. So Professor Idowu, of Nigeria, concludes his text on African traditional religions by saying, "We maintain that [African traditional religion] is *the* religion of the majority of Africans today. We can add that there is every indication that the process of modernization, and of syncretism with the [traditional] religion as the senior and predominant element in the mixture, will continue" (1973:208, his emphasis).

To a certain extent this is understandable and perhaps praiseworthy. Indeed theologians from other parts of the Third World have watched this process with admiration. The official statement of Third World Theologians meeting in 1977 contains a tribute to African theology. In spite of the invasion from the north, "African cultures conserve their vitality," and "traditional beliefs give support for the continuing struggle to create a human society and just forms of organization" (Teologia Desde, 1982:31–32, 35).

But as Idowu's panegyric demonstrates, too much was sometimes claimed for traditional belief. Evangelical theologians in particular reacted against this excess. The first and most strident warning came from Byang Kato in his *Theological Pitfalls in Africa* (1975). While he may have been unjust in some of his criticisms, especially of John Mbiti (see Mbiti's discussion in Appiah-Kubi and Torres, 1979:85), his concerns were well founded. He sounded an important caution about the danger of universalism implicit in the return to traditional religions.

But, for his part, he could see no positive value in the study of traditional faiths. His study of his own Jaba people (of Nigeria) led him to this conclusion: "The dominating fears and superstitions concerning the spirit world are so dreadful that an instantaneous and complete cure is what the Jaba people need" (1975:38). On the other hand, he could not believe that one's understanding of the Gospel could be made any clearer by a dialogue with this other world. "The gospel content, of course," he insisted, "needs no addition or modification. It is because of this irreducible immutable message, that Christianity has produced the third race comprising men and women of all races" (ibid., 178).

The problem with presenting African culture in such a negative light, as we have seen, is that it leaves African Christians hanging in the air (the phrase is from Cyril Okorocha). Are they no longer African? In fairness to Kato, we must recognize how much has been learned about culture and its role in missions since he wrote his book (and one of the great tragedies of evangelical theology in Africa is that he died before these discussions had progressed very far). A recent book that reflects this progress is Richard Gehman's study *Doing African Christian Theology* (1987). Here a much more positive role is given to culture in the communication of the gospel, and his study includes a most helpful historical survey of changing attitudes toward culture among Christians in Kenya. But even here the assumption seems to be that theology, and not just Scripture, is authoritative across cultures. Africans need to hear, he insists, that "salvation is by grace through faith alone, even though this concept was foreign to their culture and strange to their ears" (ibid., 84). For "it would appear to me that the very structure of Systematic Theology is influenced by Scripture itself" (85). This leads him to the view that "Christians lapse into their traditional religion because they are weak in faith and weak faith is due to a lack of biblical teaching" (110).

While no one would dispute the truth of this, Cyril Okorocha discusses another important cause for a return to traditional faith among Christians. A major problem, he argues in his 1987 dissertation, is that Christianity too often leaves people hanging, "rooted out of one value-system and not wholly fitted into the other" (1987:13). The debate, he insists, is not merely over the cultural adaptation of Christianity, but it is also a religio-cultural interaction. "When cultural institutions are divested of their ontological religious significance [people] can no longer hear or answer the voice of Christ in context" (28). Another Nigerian theologian, Osadolor Imasogie, has concurred with this. He argues that Christians return to traditional practices because the "word did not become flesh in the African environment and consequently the Eternal Christ could not be existentially apprehended" (1983:69).

Okorocha argues, as we have seen, that for the Igbo the primal sense of the nature of salvation as *ezi-ndu*, the viable life, was decisive both in their discarding the older, now-impotent gods and the opting for the new and more powerful God of Christianity (234). Thus when Christians revert to former practices, it is because their new faith is not seen to rest on values fundamental to their identity as people—it is finally a borrowed faith. Of course it is true that Scripture in turn will provide a corrective for these expectations as, by the Holy Spirit, it exercises its transforming influence. Okorocha would certainly admit this, though it may be that his study gives this aspect less attention than it deserves.

The search for identity then, in the religious context of Africa, is clearly a theological quest. If our premise is correct, that each region of the world will have its own unique contribution to make to theological discussion, then the response that African theologians have given to this search is important not only for Africa, but also for the world. Let us see how this might be so.

Here we return to the argument that Kwame Bediako makes in his comparative study of African theologians and the theology of the early church (1983). There he makes the point that the missionary in Africa insisted on a European standard for genuine Christianity. But is there no other way to measure emergent Christianity than by European criteria? The mistake here is not merely one of cultural blindness, it is a serious theological mistake that Paul and the early Christians wrestled with. In the New Testament Paul worried that Judaism was being made into a normative framework for the Gospel. Similarly in Africa a religious system, European Christianity, has been made to challenge Paul's assessment that all people (and thus all cultures) are under God's judgment. At the same time it hides the fact that God's righteousness applies to all without exception (1983:305). The missionary felt bound "to deny the Akan world view, not only on the ground of what was essentially Christian belief, but on the ground of what was, in effect, a European world view" (ibid., 309).

The universal character of the Gospel lies in the fact that it tests all cultures, but also in the fact that it allows every people to make their contribution to the kingdom of God (ibid., 311). Western missions in Africa, Bediako concludes, in putting a different standard on African cultures than they did on their own, was a judaizing enterprise (313). Many Western missionaries were saying that to become Christians meant to take on particular cultural practices, and not only to come to Christ. Paul in Galatians makes it clear that this is "another gospel."

This critical reminder of the universal claims of the Gospel may allow us not only to reread our own Western theology critically, but it may throw fresh light on the history of theology. African theologians are insisting that unless Christianity relates to the primal values of the people, it will not take root and may eventually be discarded.

Mercy Oduyoye applies this insight to certain critical moments in church history. The Donatist Christians of North Africa (fourth to sixth centuries), for example, may have eventually gone over to Islam because Christianity did not seem to take seriously Berber spirituality. The Donatists reflected this spirituality by insisting that priests must be pure to administer the sacraments properly. If they had lapsed under persecution and were allowed to remain in the Church, they would pass on their pollution to others. Cyprian and others claimed that the sacraments were God's gifts and therefore had value regardless of the character of the administrant.

Oduyoye argues that Cyprian and Augustine both brought a Roman understanding of law and guilt and so could not fathom the depth of the spirituality they encountered in North Africa. She points out, "To the Berbers, sin (in this case apostasy) was contagious and should not be trifled with. The Church is *de facto* holy, that is made up of good women and men" (1986:23). Because their faith could not be made compatible with this fundamental intuition, Oduyoye insists, Christianity soon disappeared from North Africa (though the Donatist church did survive for several centuries, it eventually succumbed to Islam). It is interesting that throughout Africa today it is not uncommon, especially for older Christians, to refuse to receive communion from priests or ministers known to be immoral or corrupt.

But Oduyoye points to more positive examples as well. Nile Basin (Ethiopian) Christianity may have survived because it reflected the primal religion of that region (ibid., 23). In any case she concludes, "The gospel has to be dynamically related to a people's 'primal religion,' if they are to be brought to Christ" (ibid.). Could it be that this perception can give insight to the theological discussions in our own Western history? For example, could the importance we have given certain emphases—like "justification by faith"—relate to certain funda-mental expectations of our Western heritage (see on this Krister Stendahl, 1976:78–96)?

However important African theology's preoccupation with culture has been, we must hold open the possibility that it has obscured other equally important issues. There are two problems here. One is that the undeviating attention given to traditional values does not encourage honest assessment of how seriously the modern educated African takes these values. Even to ask this question is taken to imply that these beliefs are unimportant. But one does not have to be an anthropologist to see that there is a serious clash of value systems in Africa today, and a simple return to the past may not be possible or even desirable. Clearly, traditional values have shown amazing resilience, and one could argue that their role is increasing even in the cities. But educated Africans are facing a complex world. Some of my students have wondered whether this first generation of theologians—e.g., Mbiti and Idowu—were not raised in a much more homogenous culture than exists today and therefore have unrealistic hopes for the influence of these values. And more recent assessments of African theology have encouraged a more selective use of traditional religions (cf. Fashole-Luke, 1981:408: "What is needed . . . is the study of African Traditional Religion in the dimensions of space and time").

But this relates to the second problem. Almost every reference we have seen by African theologians to moderniza-tion or urbanization has been negative. The process of development has been almost universally seen as destructive to the African soul. And a return or recovery of traditional values has been seen, at least in part, as the major response that Christians are called to make. We will ask in our conclusion how realistic such antimodernizing movements are. But there is a larger question facing African Christians: What positive role will the church play in modernization? Up until the present it seems that only the secular philosophers and commentators have focused positively on the influence of modern values. Kwasi Wiredu argues that Africa must make use of modern science. And Ali Mazrui lays out the agenda for Africa in the next generation in *The African Condition*. He notes, "When this century does indeed stagger out in sheer exhaustion, ethnicity in Africa should have declined, the state system might have gotten stronger and more consolidated, ideology more sophisticated and enriched, and religion on the defensive" (1980:93; see also Wiredu, 1980).

But where are the Christian theologians who will discuss these concerns? Have Christian theologians been afraid that by discussing these things positively they might appear to be siding with colonial values? These issues may represent the agenda for theology in Africa until the year 2000. Desmond Tutu has recognized this need. He notes that African theology has succeeded in healing the African soul, but

> it has by and large failed to speak meaningfully in the face of the plethora of contemporary problems which assail modern Africa. It has seemed to advocate disengagement from the hectic business of life, because very little has been offered that is pertinent, say, about the theology of power in the face of the epidemic of coups and military rule . . . [and] other equally urgent present day issues. (in Parratt, ed. 1987:54)

As he goes on to point out, it may be that more abrasive theologies, such as liberation theology, may be more appropriate to these issues. He reminds us that there are theologians in Africa concerned with these questions, though they are to be found largely in southern Africa.

In that region, in fact, theologians have tended to be critical of what we have called African theology, considering it a distraction from the real issues facing Africa. There theologians argue that the discussion needs to be broadened to include themes that have so far been neglected. The problem with a focus on the African worldview, Manas Buthelezi says, is that it is often isolated from African people as they exist today. This context is irrelevant if Africans are not given the material and spiritual means to be themselves. "To be a person means to have power to be truly a person; it means power for liberation to be a person" (in Torres and Fabella, eds., 1978:65,

68). But to consider this approach to theology we will turn to Latin America, where these questions have been raised most forcefully.

In spite of these provisions, it is clear that the contribution of African theology is already secure. Finding one's cultural soul is not a small thing. And the refusal to allow this question to be slighted may be one of Africa's enduring legacies. African theologians have helped us see the importance of the intuitive and celebrative dimensions of faith, and its depth of mystery. They have helped us see that what cannot be verbalized may still be danced or sung. And most of all they have shown us the meaning of life lived in the presence of God and of each other. An old African proverb, with equivalents in many languages, says that one is human only because of others, with others, and for others. If we are listening, John Taylor tells us, we might learn from Africa that the least each of us owes to the other is to be completely present, just as God is present to his creation (1963:196).

3

LATIN AMERICAN THEOLOGY: CHRISTIANITY AND ITS POLITICAL SETTING

July 15 1955. The birthday of my daughter Vera Eunice. I wanted to buy a pair of shoes for her, but the price of food keeps us from realizng our desires. Actually we are slaves to the cost of living. I found a pair of shoes in the garbage, washed them, and patched them for her to wear . . . I don't have one cent to buy bread. So I washed three bottles and traded them to Arnaldo. He kept the bottles and gave me bread. Then I went to sell my paper. I received 65 cruzeiros. I spent 20 cruzeiros for meat. I got one kilo of ham and one kilo of sugar and spent six cruzeiros on cheese. And the money was gone. . . . I was ill all day. I thought I had a cold. At night my chest pained me. I started to cough. I decided not to go out at night to look for paper. I searched for my son Joao. He was at Felisberto de Carvalho Street near the market. A bus had knocked a boy into the sidewalk and a crowd gathered. Joao was in the middle of it all. I poked him a couple of times and within five minutes he was home (Diary of Carolina Maria de Jesus, 1962:17)

INTRODUCTION: WHY IS THERE SUCH MISERY?

In Africa theologians are drawn to issues of culture and identity. Starting from a setting that is in many ways similar, many Latin American theologians wrestle with social and political issues. As the Seoul Declaration of Evangelical Theologians put it in 1983: Latin American theologians "will have to forge theology from within a context in which the social, economic and political structures are in a state of disarray, unable to close the gap between the rich and the poor and to solve the problems created by economic and technologi-cal dependence. . . . Theology will have to give priority to problems relating to justice and peace" (1983:11).

In a sense these issues relate to the larger question of how Christianity can find a home outside Europe and North America. As Orlando Costas put this: "A fundamental question facing Christians in the 3rd World today is that of affirming faith in Christ without breaking their religio-cultural ties" (1982:120). This means, in all areas made the object of Western missions, making the local reality in all its dynamics the starting point of theological reflection. Where in Africa the issues of this dynamic were largely related to values and identity, in Latin America they relate to power and domina-tion. Although theology in Latin America is the heir of a longer tradition and therefore more sophisticated, there is a shared sense among Latins that they relate to the modern world from "the underside of history," that is, from a situation of powerlessness. In Latin America science, technology, and trade patterns are readily addressed, but they are addressed from the point of view of the "victims" of these forces. These realities are described from the point of view of exploited workers in a banana plantation, rather than that of the manager of the transnational company that owns the plantation.

So faith is seen to begin with this sense of powerlessness. Whereas in Africa theology began with a shout of joy, in Latin America it takes its impetus from a cry of despair. It is the voice of a people in extremis. If the poverty of the people in Latin America is no greater than in other places, it is more inescapable. Urbanization is more pervasive and cruel—by the year 2000, 75 percent of the 600 million people in the continent will live in cities. And so the cry has gone up: Why is there such misery?

In many ways liberation theology is an understandable response to this particular setting. And we will take it as the characteristic theology of this region, though we recognize at once that this term covers a wide variety of theologies and has called forth a wide range of reactions. While taking note of the varieties, we will seek to focus on common themes of these theologians in order to ask: How do these conversations contribute to the theological enterprise? Then we will take note of the reactions to liberation theology and see how these might contribute to a more balanced perspective.

The most remarkable characteristic of liberation theology is the controversy it has engendered, both inside and outside Latin America. For some, liberation theology is the only possible Christian way of responding to Latin American realities; for others it is the most serious perversion of the Gospel in our century. Since the issues are so important and the rhetoric so strident, it is necessary to put the discussion in its larger historical setting. This is particularly appropriate in Latin America, where historical issues are of the essence of theology.

Since we are particularly interested in evangelical responses to this theology, it may be appropriate to look briefly at the Protestant heritage in Latin America. Beginning in the 1850s Protestant missionaries began work in many countries of Latin America. By World War I they had established churches in all the republics of Central and South America. But their numbers were small, perhaps 500,000 out of 60 million Christians, in what was a continent domininated by Catholicism (Neill, 1964:391).

In many respects the Protestants (or *evangelios*, as they are called) were already in the nineteenth century identified with the issues of justice and the democratic spirit (Miguez, 1975:10–11; Escobar, 1987:11–12). Perhaps this was partly a result of their minority status—with 80 to 95 percent of the people identifying themselves as Catholics. Rubem Alves notes wryly, "It is understandable that [Protestants] . . . applauded with enthusiasm the republican cause, the separation of church and state, as well as any similar developments that would diminish the power of the catholicism which crushed them" (in Richard, ed., 1981:347).

But there were positive reasons for the Protestant concern for justice. While nineteenth-century Catholicism had not yet joined the modern world, Protestants were busy shaping it. The evangelical revivals of Britain and America were to have profound influence not only on the missionary movement but also on the developing modern world. The call to conversion, to new life, as José Miguez-Bonino points out, was already a subversive element in Latin American traditional society (in Richard, ed. 1985:243–347). Samuel Escobar, in his excellent discussion of these issues, adds that it was the call to personal conversion that first promised the peasants dignity. "There is no political ideology," he points out, "without a spiritual experience" (1987:20). In these ways one could argue that the Protestants provided one of the antecedents of liberation theology.

Not that there were no antecedents to this evangelical spirituality within the Catholic tradition. One must recall the important mystical tradition represented by Teresa of Avila and John of the Cross. These were certainly influential in Latin America as well, as John Mackay points out. But this was a spirituality the Protestants were to champion.

But there were liabilities associated with the Protestants' minority status. Of necessity much of their energies had to be invested in defending themselves against the persecution of the Catholic Church, so that little time or thought was given to constructive theological work. For these and other reasons, René Padilla concluded in 1971 that the evangelical church in Latin America was a church without a theology. Because of the long-standing divorce between evangelism and theology (imported from overseas?) and the concentration on numerical growth, Padilla concluded that the Gospel did not become incarnated in Latin American culture (with the resulting loss of second- and third-generation Christians. See 1972:1–6). For whatever reason, the evangelical church, while active evangelistically, was not poised to take theological leadership.

Clearly the initiative, theologically, since World War II has been with the Catholic Church. Nourished on the burgeoning Scripture studies within the Catholic Church and picking up on issues that Protestants had long championed—justice, the needs of the poor, freedom—and profiting from a new openness in the church, Catholic theologians were able to open creative avenues for theological discussion. Even in biblical studies, Samuel Escobar admits, liberation theologians have produced more substantial work than the Protestants before them (1987:137).

BACKGROUND AND DEVELOPMENT OF LIBERATION THEOLOGY

Why have theologians in Latin America focused on political and economic issues? Surely poverty is no worse there than in many places in Asia and Africa, and injustice no more striking. The answer seems to lie in the perception of her history that Latin Americans have come to hold. Whereas in Africa a rereading of history raised issues for theological discussion, in Latin America this history itself has become a theological problem.

Enrique Düssel, the major historian of liberation theology, describes Latin Americans as always being outside their own history: their Latin American history has been written by others (1974:3). More than that, he has argued, this history was shaped by conceptions that were Greek, foreign not only to Latin America but also to biblical thinking. Here he takes a tack that has become a major part of liberation theology's critique of traditional theology. For the Greeks, he points out, reality lay in the idea, so they were never able to get beyond the anecdotal in history (Düssel, 1976:19–20). This was institutionalized in the form of Constantinian Christianity, which was defined in the Middle Ages as the earthly shadow of the heavenly form. Such confidence in their Christian civilization led naturally to the Crusades against the Moors and to the conquest of Latin America. "It is a single process; it is the same Latin, Hispanic Christendom which came to America" (1974:15). This way of seeing history raises for Latins major questions not only about the nature of Christianity, as in Africa, but also about its political function.

Periods in the History of Latin America

Düssel has described three major periods in Latin American history (1974, further refined in Richard, ed., 1981:401–39):

1. *Colonial Period (1492-1808).* Christianity came to Latin America with the *conquistadores* with a unique theory of "evangelization": the conquest of Latin America was a just war waged against infidels by divine right and based on pontifical bulls (ibid.:404). To facilitate this crushing weight of authority, political control was exercised from Europe by a patronage system. Large plots of land were donated to families of *conquistadores* and formed into *encomiendas*—large plantations owned by Spanish landlords and worked by native Indians who were "baptized" and pressed into service. The oppressive character of the system aroused the conscience of some of the missionaries. One, Bartolme de las Casas, even succeeded in getting a law passed against the encomienda system in 1542. Although the law was never enforced, Las Casas has been celebrated as one of the antecedents of liberation ideology.

Most of the Indians were baptized, but the mission was conducted "with little reference to historical factors which would make their efforts worthwhile" (Julio Barreiro in Santa Ana, ed., 1978:128). As their Aztec and Inca narratives were ignored and their ruins pillaged, the indigenous people were scarcely influenced by Christianity. Miquez Bonino sums up the attitude of many toward this colonial period: "What was established in Latin America was not a Latin American church, but a Spanish church transplanted, together with its liturgy, buildings, laws, feasts, and devotions" (J. Miguez Bonino, quoted in ibid.:132).

Meanwhile, the Catholic Church allied itself entirely with the patrician class, the 5 percent who came to own 80 percent of the land. In this two-class society, the masses felt the church to be foreign and distant, while the church sacralized the existing social structure as the the earthly model of the

LATIN AMERICAN THEOLOGY

heavenly archetype. This was a church, says Miguez Bonino, that was foredoomed to reactionism (1975:5–7).

2. *Decline of Christendom—Rise of Pluralism (1808-1962)*. The nineteenth century was a time of transition from colonial rule to independence and from "sacred" to secular states. In some ways the church was beginning to respond to its context; many Latin priests were ordained. But other forces were threatening the advance of Christianity. The universities became influential centers of nationalistic ideals, throwing over Catholic scholastic theology for nineteenth century positivism imported from Europe. The political orientation of Latin America was encouraged by the fact that, in contrast to Africa, virtually all the states had already achieved independence by 1900 and cities by this time had already become highly developed. The stage was being set for political and theological discussions that were to come.

José Miguez Bonino emphasizes especially the rise of Anglo-American neocolonialism during this period. Instead of being ruled from ecclesiastical centers in Europe, Latin America became the pawn of board rooms in Britain and America. The fact of dependence remained the same whether the regime was colonial or neocolonial: "The basic fact of the determination of all our economy and development by the needs of the masters prevailing at the time is in all cases the same" (1975:14).

Following World War II, Anglo-American–sponsored programs such as the much-touted Alliance for Progress raised great hopes for economic growth. There was optimistic talk about capital and technology transfer and about the possibility that Latin America would reach the take-off point for economic growth that northern countries had reached one hundred years previously. And in fact from 1950 to 1961 foreign investment totaled $9.6 billion—though during this same period $14.4 billion was repatriated (see Düssel, 1981:4). By this time, as well, the secular tradition of the universities (both in Latin America and the West) had assured that the entire development discussion was conducted within a thoroughly secular framework (see D. Goulet, 1974:9–10).

77

3. *Break with Christendom—Emergence of a New Spirit (1962 to the present).* By the early 1960s it had become clear to everyone in Latin America that "developmentalism" had failed to live up to its promises (as a result the word "development"—*desallorismo*—has come to have a negative connotation in Latin America). The economic situation was growing worse instead of better. Three-fourths of the people were still illiterate in many countries; there was vitually no inter-American trade; the extractive industries were owned by foreigners (Miguez Bonino, 1975:14–20). In fact many people began to wonder whether Latin American underdevelopment might not be the necessary underside of northern development. An important component of liberation theology was the development during this time of the dependency theory of economics. Working at the Latin America Study Center in Chile (CEPAL), F. H. Cardos and E. Falletto began to raise questions about the reigning developmental theory.

According to thinking behind programs like the Alliance for Progress, regular economic growth could be encouraged by large investment in industrial facilities. The benefits of the resulting growth would "trickle down" to the poorer segments of society. But the facts failed to support the theory—the poorer classes were growing and their situation was deteriorating. Scholars at CEPAL began to argue that dependency and thus also underdevelopment were not merely a temporary condition but a necessary consequence of present economic structures. Any real progress would entail a radical break from the situation of economic dependency (cf. J. B. Libanio, 1987:35).

Marxist thought was important to all this, but it is possible to overemphasize its role. In fact there was a gathering social impatience and yearning for liberation from centuries of oppression, quite outside any ideological framework. Students in the 1960s were often the first to articulate these longings. They claimed, "Our whole culture, whatever the intention in constructing it might have been, was working for the benefit of the ruling classes" (Segundo, 1983:3). It is certainly true that

Marxists exploited this dissatisfaction, but it is false to say they created it.

This point needs to be stressed. Prior to any particular expression of liberation theology, there was already an ongoing social revolution caused by rising expectations and frustrated hopes. Already in 1969, Protestant Rubem Alves could write about the birth of a new language and a new community: Humanity is "determined to liberate himself historically" (1969:5, 11). And a few years later Gustavo Gutiérrez, often called the father of liberation theology, wrote: "The point of departure of our theological reflection is the process of liberation in Latin America. More concretely, it is engagement in this process which Latin Americans are assuming" (writing in 1972, quoted in Miguez Bonino, 1975:42).

This continent-wide discontent with economic developments spawned student movements in cities and guerrilla movements throughout the countryside, many including priests and even pastors. These were giving expression to legitimate yearnings for a better life that must be seen as an important antecedent to liberation theology. It was partly these valid aspirations, combined with the absence of a constructive theology, that led evangelicals like John Stam and Orlando Costas to defend liberation theology more strongly than they might otherwise have done (though even these would not want themselves to be called simply liberation theologians).

The Rise of Liberation Theology

Liberation theology as a theological movement arose from the interaction between this cultural ferment in Latin America and the newer winds blowing in Roman Catholicism. Vatican II, meeting from 1961 to 1965, was called by Pope John XXIII to bring the church up to the present. And with its talk of the church as the people of God, its emphasis on Scripture study, and its strong statements about social justice, it did actually open new areas of discussion on the mission of the church (Miguez Bonino in fact calls it the decisive entrance of the Catholic Church into the modern world, 1975:17; Düssel, by contrast, sees Vatican II as still being under the influence of the bourgeois worldview, Richard, ed., 1981:423–424).

Vatican II also exerted certain theological and philosophical influences that were to become important—expressive perhaps of the bourgeois views Düssel rejects. Clodovis Boff points out that the emphasis on opening up earthly realities for their own sake came from the influence of Teilhard de Chardin. This became evident in particular in the document "Gaudium and Spes" on the church in the modern world. This in turn influenced the Medellín documents, which "have opened the field for the theology of liberation" (C. Boff, 1987:235n16).

In 1968 the Latin American bishops met in Medellín, Colombia, for what was to be a momentous conference. Building on what had been done during Vatican II, the bishops spoke of the failure of developmentalism and the need for liberation from dependency: "We refer here to the consequences of the dependence of our countries from a center of economic power around which they gravitate. From this it results that our nations are not masters of their own resources and economic decisions. Obviously this is not without effects on the political realm" (bishops' statement quoted in Miguez Bonino 1975:27). That such a progressive statement should come, not from a few theologians, but from the pastors of the Latin American church was to have profound impact.

The first actual statement of liberation theology came in 1969 when the Peruvian priest and theologian Gustavo Gutiérrez gave a paper in Switzerland entitled "A Theology of Liberation." There he proposed that theology should work with a new paradigm—one that would replace older developmental or reform models, that of liberation. In what amounted to an outline of his 1971 (ET 1973) book, he confessed he had come to three decisive conclusions:
1. Poverty is a destructive thing that must be fought against.
2. Poverty is not a result of chance; it results from unjust structures.

3. Poor people are a social class. "It became crystal clear that in order to serve the poor, one had to move into political action" (quoted in Brown, 1978:61–62).
These propositions in fact were felt to be so important and so inescapable that they should become the starting point for all theological reflection—what Juan Segundo was later (in 1976) to call the necessary pretheoretical commitment of theology in Latin America.

In Latin America the publication of Gutiérrez' book and the discussion it engendered was met with widespread enthusiasm. Mortimer Arias, the Methodist bishop of Bolivia and later the rector of the Biblical Seminary of Costa Rica, notes that liberation theology was met in the 1970s with something of the same euphoria that greeted the Alliance for Progress in the 50s. But these later hopes, like the earlier ones, were soon to be dashed. In the course of the latter decade military strongmen, in the name of national security, took over in several countries. Naturally liberation theology became the object of attack, and many of its leaders were imprisoned or exiled (Arias, 1980:22–25).

This crisis led to what Segundo has called the *second phase* of liberation theology. The violent opposition led theologians to a deep reevaluation. The many popular movements for liberation appeared to care nothing for liberation theology. What after all had it accomplished? Many of the proponents of liberation theology began to wonder if the theologians didn't need a kind of liberation themselves. Perhaps liberation theology had been too much the product of theologians, perhaps it needed to be relocated within the mind of the common people. Led by Brazilian priests Dom Helder Camara and Leonardo Boff, liberation theologians came to identify themselves—often actually relocating to poor areas— as a ministry by and for the brokenhearted, a voice of the voiceless (see Segundo, 1983:5–10).

Just as some of the earlier triumphalism was dissipating (and with it some of the more violent and revolutionary connotations), political events were giving liberation thinkers some cause for encouragement. The emphasis of the Carter presidency on human rights was welcomed everywhere in Latin America, and the triumph of the Sandinistas in Nicaragua raised people's hopes that foreign and oppressive power could be thrown off. In accordance with this new orientation, emphasis was given to the growing "Base Communities" as the source of reflection, and a spirituality that truly reflected the aspirations of the people. By the early 1980s these developments had given liberation theology a second wind and new worldwide visibility.

Before I make some comment on this history it may be appropriate to note some of the varieties of theologies of liberation that have developed. Samuel Escobar divides them roughly into three types, from the most radical to the more conservative. The radical theologians, made up of professors and academics, are more open to Marxist categories both in social analysis and in hermeneutics. They include people like Assman, Pixley, and Sergio Arce. In the moderate group are those Escobar calls pastoral theologians. These are more concerned with the life of the people in their daily concerns and take the Scriptures more seriously. These are represented by Gutiérrez, Segundo, and Leonardo Boff, who take liberation theology in a more evangelical direction. Finally, there are the populists who emphasize popular religiosity and tend to be critical of both Marxism and capitalism. Escobar likens this group to Polish Christianity and the present pope, but with a liberationist caste. They are represented by Juan Carlos Scannone and Lucio Gera (Escobar, 1987:193–195).

Has Liberation Theology Misread Its History?

Needless to say, the reaction to liberation theology both inside and outside Latin America was immediate and strident, though the resulting discussion has often produced more heat than light. Large groups of Catholics (represented by the Opus Dei and the Cursillists) have been indifferent or opposed to liberation theology; the large and influential charismatic movement has usually been critical, feeling that it has made no impact on spirituality, i.e., on the renewal of the church. On the Protestant front, the largest and fastest-growing Pentecostal churches, though they are usually the poor, have not shared this revolutionary consciousness. In general, evangelicals, especially those with ties to North America, have been highly critical (though there have been significant exceptions: Orlando Costas and Juan Stam have been basically supportive and Samuel Escobar and René Padilla have been critically sympathetic). Let us look with some care at the discussion this particular reading of history has engendered.

On the one hand, there are those observers who believe liberation theology is basically a development of ideas previously circulating in Europe or America and therefore not really an original contribution to theology. Some see this positively as an expression of a perennial impulse of Christianity. John C. Bennett believes that "Liberation theology today is in some respects in a line of succession from such representatives of the Social Gospel as Walter Rauschenbusch. The Social Gospel was a theology of liberation for the industrial workers of this country" (quoted in Brown, 1987:167). Ronald White has proposed in conversation that the old Student Christian Movement in Latin America may have been the mediator of some of these ideas, though, as René Padilla pointed out to me, there is a generation missing between this influence and the rise of liberation theology.

Others are more critical of this outside influence and accuse liberation theology of depending on a "seminar Marxism" that shows us nothing peculiar to Latin America. Jürgen Moltmann has made this point in an article in 1976. One would like to discover Latin America in Gutiérrez, he says, but one is disappointed. "One reads more about the sociological theories of others, namely, western sociologists, than about the history of the life and suffering of Latin American people" (1976:60). Perhaps the second phase of liberation theology has recognized this weakness and made more contact with the people. But as Christine Gudorf points out, one can hardly blame Latin theologians for using terminology of Western thinkers, for they wish to be a part of the worldwide theological discussion and not simply to reflect their own setting. The very idea of dependency requires one to address the subjects of this oppression. It is doubtful, she concludes, if these writers would be taken seriously if they had "only referred to unknown Latin writers and to communities of illiterate *campesinos*" (Gudorf, 1987:10).

Then there are those who see this reading of Latin history as simply wrong, or at least oversimplified. The first group is represented by British economist Brian Griffiths, who believes that the dependency theory is really an extension of classic British Fabianism and Lenin's theory of Imperialism. Underdevelopment cannot be blamed on external factors alone; it must be understood in terms of indigenous obstacles, whether cultural or historical. Griffiths concludes, "In general terms I believe that the charge which these people make [underdevelopment rests on oppressive economic structures] is almost entirely untrue" (1982:130).

Samuel Escobar, while sympathetic with some of the emphases of liberation theology, believes its reading of history is oversimplified. There was exploitation and pillage on the part of missionaries; and there is injustice in present trade patterns. But Miguez Bonino's idea of two colonialisms "is a dangerous simplification which tends to hide certain facts which are very important to understand the present ideological and political alternatives" (1987:113).

This kind of criticism needs to be heard, but I wonder if much of it (especially that emanating from North America) doesn't miss the point. No people's history is a transcript of "things as they actually are" (von Ranke); historians in general reject this standard of nineteenth-century historiography. History is rather a people telling their story. In Latin America the sense that for centuries the people have been pawns in a game played by others, has become widespread. Moreover there is a growing consensus that people, if liberated from oppression, can begin to take responsibility for their own future. Interestingly the most bitter critiques of this story come from the North. This is as might be expected, for the point of this Latin story is that the way one sees things is determined by the social and political place in which one stands. Does it make no difference that Latin history has been told up to now by those who held power over the region—either politically or economically?

What if this same history is told by the people who have suffered under the hardships? How would it sound in this case? Under the leadership of Enrique Düssel and Pablo Richard a vast and scholarly program has been launched with just this purpose in view (see Richard, ed., 1981 and 1985). Richard explains that these scholars have set out "to reconstruct the historical memory of the people of God in Latin America" (1985:xi). This is important not only for the identity of this people, as it was in Africa, but also to enable them to participate as agents in their future (ibid.:19).

Perhaps it is difficult for us who have such different backgrounds to appreciate the importance of this recasting of history by Latin Americans. Before we dismiss it as reductionist we need to ask whether our social situation has no influence on the way we think as Christians. It ought at least to give us pause when someone like Orlando Costas points out "that as far back as William Carey and as recently as [the Lausanne movement] the financial backbone of a lot of the churches and missionary societies that we [evangelicals] represent is to be found among those who possessed wealth, knowledge, and power, indeed among those who control" (Samuel and Sugden, eds., 1983:6–7, his emphasis). He goes on to ask: will this have no impact on the way we understand the work of Christ? What about those who see things from the point of view of powerlessness, how will they see Christ?

At the very least we will have to listen carefully to those who believe the answers to these questions are important. We would not be honest if we did not ask questions in return. But first we turn to a careful examination of the new way of doing theology that this history has suggested.

A NEW WAY OF DOING THEOLOGY?

The Hermeneutical Circle

To understand liberation theologians we must at least take seriously their claim that this reading of history leads to a new way of doing theology. Previously, they insist, theology has been done from the point of view of the observer; now it will be done from the point of view of one engaged in a particular historical project. Because of the influence of Greek philosophy, the movement in theology has been from theory to practice; now theology must be understood as reflection on practice. This leads them to develop a unique form of the hermeneutical circle.

Theology, according to liberation theology, always begins in a particular social and historical situation. This is its necessary *starting point.* Consistent with current assumptions in sociology of knowledge, they insist that all thought arises out of a social context and inevitably bears the marks of that setting. Juan Segundo elaborates this thesis: "Everything involving ideas is intimately bound up with the existing social situation in at least an unconscious way" (1976:8). Since there is no such thing as "autonomous knowledge"—that is, knowledge that is totally unrelated to the situation of the knower, the existing circumstances must be accepted consciously as the starting point for theological reflection.

This setting becomes a part of the presuppositions that we bring to Scripture. A generation ago German theologian Rudolf Bultmann argued that all interpretation is influenced by pretheoretical factors. But whereas Bultmann, coming from a Western tradition, was interested in the existential self-understanding that determines our reading of Scripture, liberation theology directs its attention to the social and political self-understanding or commitment. For liberation theology this pretheoretical commitment must then include a *precommitment to liberation.*

For many observers of liberation theology, this jump from social setting to a commitment to liberation is one of the most difficult aspects to understand and accept. But it is an essential step in their hermeneutical circle, and so we must consider it carefully. On one level it appears to be a "gut conviction" that the general situation in Latin America calls forth. The reading of history has led to a consensus that the present situation has become intolerable and that something must be done about it. As Miguez Bonino points out, this is not so much an insistence on some particular political order as it is an insistence on the nonnecessity of this particular situation (1983:90).

But on a broader front one has to keep in mind the reality of the social movement toward liberation surging through Latin America (a movement that predated, remember, the rise of liberation theology). As evangelical Sidney Rooy points out: "That a social revolution is taking place in Latin America is an indisputable fact of our time" (1986:60). If this fact is assumed, the real question becomes not whether to take sides, but which side to take. Rooy believes that "the response of the Church to the social revolution in our lands will determine its future" (ibid.:89).

To those of us living in the North, where political choices are far less urgent, this push to take sides seems overdrawn— perhaps because we enjoy situations of privilege that don't call for redress. We go to the polls and follow with interest the results on TV, but the outcome is seldom a life-and-death issue for us. Meanwhile we enjoy the benefits of a balance of political powers, recourse to the courts, and a strong labor movement. We can afford to feel relaxed. In many places of Latin America the situation demands much more immediate and far-reaching decisions. The political choice is forced—in much the same way that a German who faced at his doorstep a Jew fleeing from the Nazis during World War II was forced to make a political choice with life-and-death consequences. To side with the process of liberation seems, to Latin Americans, to have just this kind of urgency.

The next step can be seen to grow out of this precommitment. If we always read Scripture from a particular social location, theologians in Latin America have chosen to read it from within the commitment to liberation. Given the pre-

involvement in the social movement, Christians are called to *reread Scripture in the light of this commitment.* This is a very important step in the circle. Again this is quite different from the circle that Bultmann proposed. There the play was between the reading of Scripture and my existential self-understanding; in liberation theology the circle goes back and forth between the past readings of Scripture and those of the present. New understandings of history (and new commitments) lead to a suspicion of previous understandings and a rereading of Scripture. The commitment to liberation then becomes important to what one perceives in Scripture. Segundo argues, "Partiality is justified because we must find, and designate as the word of God, that part of divine revelation which *today*, in the light of our concrete historical situation, is most useful for the liberation to which God summons us" (1976:33, his emphasis).

The final step, then, is the obedience that is engendered by this rereading of Scripture. The important point is that, according to liberation theology, *truth is discovered only in practice.* Again Segundo says, "The truth is truth only when it serves as the basis for truly human attitudes. 'Doers of the truth' is the formula used by divine revelation to stress the priority of orthopraxis over orthodoxy when it comes to truth and salvation" (he is discussing James Cone, but with approval; ibid.:32). Notice that the reading of Scripture is meant not only to illumine our understanding but also to stimulate further practice, for "the praxis of liberation is thus considered the criterion for determining the truth of a particular theology" (Volf, 1983:15).

There is a biblical ring to this insistence on doing the truth. We may even agree that political precommitments are a part of the presuppositions we bring to Scripture and that they influence what we find there. But liberation theology goes beyond this to insist that some particular political commitment, namely, the commitment to liberation, is necessary to a "true" reading of Scripture.

We are faced here with the very difficult issue of the theoretical status of presuppositions. Recognizing that presuppositions are unavoidable, how are they to be evaluated? We may agree that response and obedience are a prerequisite to seeing the truth of Scripture. This response may even be relatively unreflective, i.e., it may have been forced on us by the exigencies of the situation. But this does not make it value-free. Choices may be forced, but even forced choices are not privileged. They still must be critically examined in the light of our reading (or rereading of Scripture). As Andrew Kirk puts this, "The facts of exploitation are eloquent, but they are powerless to provide a motive to struggle against them" (1980:129). We will want to return to this issue below.

Praxis

We have acknowledged that the emphasis on practice is an important contribution that liberation theology is making to theological discussion. The concept of *praxis* has become a technical term that denotes the role that action plays in theology—not just any action, but action directed toward particular ends. As educationalist Paulo Freire explains, praxis is "reflection and action upon the world in order to transform it" (1972:28). Enrique Düssel, in particular, has been eloquent in defense of the importance of praxis. He points out that the Greeks, and those Western cultures influenced by them, found meaning in the "idea," or eternal truth, and thus conceived of theology as rational thought. But in Scripture it is the prophet, not the philosopher, who defines meaning. The prophet calls the people to find the significance of the present, not in the idea, but in the past actions of God. Jesus and his disciples "found the meaning and import of the present moment in the past history of their people" (1976:19). Moreover, in the New Testament this meaning could only be appropriated as one responded to Jesus' call to discipleship, to follow him—that is, to continue the project of redemption that God began in the Old Testament.

José Miguez Bonino characterizes this as *the unavoidable historical mediation* of Christian obedience" (1975:98, his emphasis). Because of our Western heritage, he says, biblical truth has been thought of as something independent of the social reality in which we are immersed, something "out there." But for us as humans there is "no truth outside or beyond the concrete historical events in which men are involved as agents" (ibid.:88). There is no knowledge outside of action. Freire elaborates this in terms of educational theory: "The unfinished character of men and the transformational character of reality necessitates that education be an ongoing activity" (1972:57).

The discussion of praxis constitutes one of liberation theology's most far-reaching and controversial contributions to theology. René Padilla is one who believes this emphasis is profoundly biblical:

> The only theology that the Bible knows is a functional theology, that is to say, a theology in dialogue with the concrete reality, a theology in the service of praxis. The only way to live an authentic Christian life is to take seriously Jesus Christ's incarnation. (in Torres in Fabella, eds., 1978:213)

Salvation has to do with God's saving actions in history, and the calling of the Christian in turn is to mediate this salvation to the world through one's life and witness. This leads to liberationists' insistence that the call to love God and one's neighbor is not an emotional attachment but a historical course of action. The call of God is to radical transformation of one's life and situation, to work performed on behalf of justice and freedom for others (see Alejandro Cussianovich, 1979:19; and Miguez Bonino, 1983:84).

Foundational to this are God's actions to restore and establish right relationships—the calling of Israel and the coming of Christ. But the fact that this work is incorporated into what is called the covenant indicates that human response has been taken up into God's program (ibid.).

In a major exegetical work, José Miranda traces the conception that God has intervened in history to establish righteousness throughout Scripture. He concludes that it is only when interhuman justice is manifest that we can say God is present. "The glory of God [is] a comprehensive, supraindividual reality which comes into human history and establishes itself there, constituting in it a new age, a universal reign of goodness and justice" (1974:239).

So the practice demanded by God is not simply our individual obedience but the formation of a society that is compatible with this reign of God. Miguez Bonino admits—in response to his critics—that this may not determine political norms, but it cannot be irrelevant to them (1983:86–90). For it is into this world that the kingdom has been introduced and where its firstfruits are poured out in the Holy Spirit.

This emphasis on obedience and discipleship may add an important dimension to theological reflection. It is true that our theology has sometimes been overintellectualized— reflecting the dominant influence of Greek philosophy. Theological truth in Scripture is meant to be "functional," to transform lives and society. Samuel Escobar, quoting Juan Mackay, notes that we have for too long had a theology of the "balcony"; we need now a theology of "road" (1987:86).

But this line of argument has its own dangers. While our understanding of truth may emerge only as we are on the way, as we are faithful to it, the reality of God and his Word is prior to that understanding. This reality may not be separable from my life in the world, but it is clearly beyond me in the prior events of Christ and in the givenness of God's self-revelation. As René Padilla explains this: we may know only to the degree we obey; but we can obey only to the degree that we know the commands and promises of God in Scripture (quoted in Escobar, 1987:98). Historical mediation may be necessary, but its meaning can be clear only in the light of God's purposes, which ultimately transcend that mediation (as Miguez Bonino himself makes clear in several places; see 1975:87, 98, 138–39, 163).

Marxist Analysis and Ideological Suspicion

One of the major innovations of liberation theology is its use of sociological analysis as a part of its theological method. As this has been the object of much criticism (and misunderstanding), it deserves careful attention. We noted that the dependency theory of economics was developed during the 1960s to counteract the prevailing developmental theories. But this development was part of wider discussions in Latin America.

To social scientists in Latin America, the failure of developmentalism was associated with the weakness of the prevailing social science models of society in the North. Social science had been taken captive, they believe, by structural and functional theories of society. These take the existing functional society as a norm and understand all change as adaptation or adjustment of the prevailing structure. This picture did not fit the harsh realities of Latin America (Miguez Bonino, 1975:34).

These realities led Latin thinkers to consider a Marxist social analysis a better interpretive tool for their situation. Marxist analysis sees society, not as a functioning organism, but as a conflictive reality. These warring elements do not call for adaptation but for major restructuring. Miguez Bonino believes that this is really a more accurate picture of human society and refers to Calvin's description of society as a battlefield of greed and self-seeking (ibid:119). The solution to this, in scriptural terms, is a radical transformation. Notice how, in the thinking of Miguez Bonino, this social analysis is chosen because it seems truer to Latin American realities, but also because it is compatible with Scripture.

This is the context in which the issue of violence must be discussed. Violence is an inevitable result of the conflicts that exist in society. Often liberation thinkers are unfairly accused of introducing the question of violence into theology. They point out that violence is a fact that must be recognized; it is a result, to put the matter in theological terms, of living in a fallen order. The facts of oppression and suffering cannot be ignored in Latin America; they constitute what Dom Heldera Camara has often called "first violence." As he says, "It must be underlined that violence already exists and that it is wielded, sometimes unconsciously, by the very people who denounce it as a scourge on society" (in Kee, ed., 1974:141).

The violence that may be necessary to liberate society is really only a just response to this reality, a response that Camara calls "redemptive violence." In fairness to liberation theology, however, the major theologians have renounced violence as inappropriate for Christians, or at least they see it as a last resort. Miguez Bonino points out, "Nonviolent action is not only most appropriate to the Christian conscience but also to the revolutionary purpose" (ibid., 127). But to ignore violence altogether is to ignore the contradictions in society that are its cause.

But why have people been able to ignore these realities for so long? Here liberation theology has made use of still another Marxist category, that of ideology. "Ideology" is any kind of theoretical justification of vested interests (see Kirk, 1980:34; Segundo, 1976:39–62). Every social order is supported by some theory that claims to justify its structure. But on the Marxist naturalistic reading of history, the real moving power of history is economic and political. Marxists have conveniently labeled religion and other theories "ideological"; that is, they rationalize—and thus hide—actual controlling interests, for example, the desire of the rich oligarchies to hold on to their power. The real dynamics of history, they believe, are the economic forces—a proposition they label scientific rather than ideological!

Although liberation thinkers are critical of this Marxist reductionism, they find the concept of "ideology" useful. For their reading of history has led them to see that the narrative they have received from the colonial writers has tended to justify (and obscure) the real motives of conquest. Thus they have used "ideological suspicion" while studying this history. Similarly, at the point of rereading Scripture, theologians have asked what vested interests previous readings of Scripture have served. Many Latin Americans believe that the history they have been taught and sometimes even the reading of Scripture they have learned have often reflected the concerns (and the questions) of the Northern contexts in which they arose. Thus it is necessary, they believe, to reread Scripture in the light of their own struggles.

But how does one make a start with this "rereading"? Obviously one needs to have a clear picture of the social situation, and this involves what has come to be called "social analysis." Since history and the social situation have been the sparks for this rethinking, liberation theology has seen the need for instruments that would help them understand these dimensions. Clearly traditional theology was not equipped to deal on this level and so Latin theologians have turned to the social sciences for help—especially sociology and, as we have seen, history.

This implies a kind of Copernican revolution in the minds of liberation theologians. Previously theologians had used philosophy as the handmaiden of theology, and theology accordingly was thought of in rational categories. Now it is clear that history is a better quarry for theological building material. Since *praxis*, rather than reflection, is the fundamental category in this realm, the sciences that study this— sociology, politics, and the sciences of culture—become the tools of choice (see the discussion in Escobar, 1987:94).

What exactly is the "social analysis" that is being called for? In order to "read" one's situation, one may make use of surveys, interviews, scholarly studies, and other means to "examine causes, probe consequences, delineate linkages and identify actors" (Holland and Henriot, 1983:8). Notice the assumption is that the discovery of the cultural, structural, and historical relationships are necessary to Christian obedience, at least in Latin America.

Now it is true that this analysis forms a part of the Marxist analysis of society, but the consensus is that this way of describing things has been chosen because it best fits the situation in Latin America. Liberationists are quick to insist that this implies no synthesis between Marxism and Christianity. Gutiérrez in fact believes the encounter is between the social sciences (which have been influenced by Marxism) and Christianity, not between Marxism and Christianity (see discussion and quotes in ibid; cf. also Miguez Bonino 1975:96–97). Miguez Bonino has written that the Marxist view of the person, lacking an understanding of sin, is finally superficial (1976): and Segundo likewise has criticized the oversimplification of Marxist sociology (1976:5-7-62).

But many critics have questioned whether the analysis that Marxism suggests can be used independently of the "ideological" framework. A strong attack on this assumption was launched by Joseph Ratzinger in the *Instruction on Liberation Theology* (1984), Rome's official response to liberation theology. There he points out that Marxists themselves believe that the analysis cannot be separated from praxis, and that there is no truth (even of analysis!) outside of the struggle of the revolutionary class. He concludes, "It is not the *fact* of social stratification, but the *theory* of class struggle as the fundamental law of history which has been accepted [by liberation theology]" (1984:22). So God himself seems to be tied to this immanentistic development.

Even more significant for our purposes has been the response of bishops in the Philippines to this use of social analysis. In the early 1980s in this Southeast Asian country there was much enthusiastic study of Marxist analysis in an attempt to understand their own setting. Gradually they became aware that there was a weakness implicit in this way of analyzing society. They concluded that this analysis was limited in the questions it asked about human communities. Specifically it does not adequately allow for the religious dimension of human development, it aims to aggravate class conflict, it tends to reduce human nature to economically determined factors, and it is intolerant of political or philosophical pluralism (D. Elwood, 1987:135). It would seem that the separation of Marxist analysis from Marxist praxis is only a theoretical one. For any analysis appears in the end to be based on certain presuppositions about the nature of society and of social change—a faith perspective must be operative here as well as later (ibid., 134, 140–41).

In their popular book *Social Analysis*, actually a manual for pastors and Christian workers, Holland and Henriot acknowledge the limitations of a purely sociological analysis. These limits, they point out, lie not in its Marxist roots, but in its heritage in Enlightenment rationalism. This has given such analysis a negative, abstractive, and elitist character (1983:89–91). But they insist that even within these limitations analysis has an important role to play in pastoral work. Indeed they insist that analysis—the one they propose includes a careful study of the people's religious values—should precede theological reflection and pastorial planning as a part of a vital pastoral circle (ibid., 8).

However understood, liberation theology reminds us that proper obedience will depend on an accurate understanding of our setting. René Padilla describes the fundamental calling Christians feel in Latin America as follows: How do we tell Maria Carolina de Jesus who lives in the slum of São Paulo that she is a child of God? In this task we may use whatever tools can help—the discovery of "interest" and "ideological suspicion" may be useful. In helping us see these realities, Padilla insists, Marxism has been helpful—and if these insights are congenial to the Christian point of view, it cannot be Christianity that is dependent on Marxism! But this must all be judged by Scripture, not the reverse. Liberation theology has rightly pointed out the ideological captivity of academic theology in the West; submitting to a Marxist captivity in Latin America leaves us in a worse situation (lecture in Berkeley, Calif., 3 March 1987).

The Preferential Option for the Poor

One of the major contributions of liberation theology has been its expounding the biblical and theological significance of the poor. In Latin America, where some 70 percent of the people are poor, theology must reflect on the significance of poverty. Thomas Hanks (1983) and Pedrito Maynard-Reid (1987) among others have shown us the central role of the poor in Scripture. And the third bishops' conference at Puebla (1979) enumerated the groups that fill out the statistics of Latin America: young children, juveniles, indigenous peoples, *campesinos*, laborers, underemployed and unemployed, the marginalized, persons living in overcrowded urban slums, the elderly—the list goes on (par. 32–39 in Boff and Boff, 1987:25).

In his classic study Gustavo Gutiérrez distinguishes three kinds of poverty. First there is material poverty, which is scandalous and must be fought against. Second, there is a spiritual poverty of those who have made themselves totally available to God as little children. But Gutiérrez goes on to elaborate a third meaning, which is called forth by the situation in Latin America: "Christian poverty, an expression of love, is solidarity *with the poor* and is protest *against poverty*" (1973:300–301, his emphasis). Christian poverty in Latin America is solidarity and protest.

So reflection on poverty in Latin America is, in the first place, a part of the necessary commitment (they would argue the precommitment) that is a prerequisite to doing theology in that setting. The Gospel must be preached and Scriptures must be read from this point of view. This line of thinking has led them to define what is called the "preferential option for the poor."

Liberation thinkers define this preference primarily in theological terms. That is, God, because of his justice and mercy, is drawn to the poor. Gustavo Gutiérrez has argued recently that the real meaning of the poor is to be found in God himself. Since God is just and people are made in his image, when this image is effaced, God's glory is hidden. God is especially concerned about the poor, Gutiérrez notes, not because they are good, but because he is good. God loves the poor because he is God (lecture at the American Academy of Religion, New York, 9 December 1984).

Orlando Costas points to a further Christological reason for giving special attention to the poor: since God came as a suffering servant and his authority was earned by suffering death, he must be known by the nonpersons of society. "Wherever there is oppression, there is the Spirit of Christ incarnated in the experience of the oppressed; there is God contextualized in the present history of the non-persons of society" (1982:13).

But this preferential option also gives the poor what is

called an "epistemological privilege"—that is, a special ability to know and understand God. The assumption is that the poor, having few resources of their own to rely on, are uniquely open to God because they are able to cry out for help without shame. In this way they will be able to apprehend something about God and his love that others cannot see.

There is little doubt that liberation theology has made a lasting contribution with its reflection on the poor—not only in methodology but in theology itself. Scripture does insist that God's ear is especially open to the poor who cry to him (Exod. 22:23), and the law is tilted in favor of the poor (Lev. 25:35–37). Christ's inaugural sermon in Luke 4:18–21 quotes from Isaiah 58 and 61: "The Spirit of the Lord has anointed me to preach good news to the poor," indicating that the deliverance of the year of jubilee is being realized and the poor are the special recipients. These and similar themes have been the object of special attention by liberation writers.

But the reductionism that threatened certain kinds of social analysis is a danger here as well. Liberation theology, in reacting against an overly spiritualized interpretation of Scripture, comes down heavily on the this-worldly quality of faith. If society is analyzed primarily in terms of social and economic dynamics, poverty will be seen primarily in these terms as well. But as Cardinal Ratzinger points out, one must not confuse the poor of Scripture with the proletariat of Marx. In the former, there is "preference given to the poor, without exclusion, whatever their form of poverty, because they are preferred by God" (1984:24). In the latter the poor are limited to the class that participates in the revolutionary struggle. But God hears the cry not only of the economically poor but also of the oppressor who cries out to be delivered from his greed. For it is just at the point of our need, whatever it might be, that Christ died for us (Rom. 5:6).

But the basic challenge of liberation theology still stands: Does this cry for deliverance have no relation to the structures that perpetuate poverty? Liberation theologians agree that Christ wants to bring about the liberation of all classes of people and that God's deliverance is primarily deliverance from sin. But in the final analysis, they insist, the rich—and the poor—will not be truly liberated as long as structural injustice is left intact. For poverty, like the sin of which it is the bitter fruit, is not merely a personal reality; it has a larger social dimension as well.

SOME THEOLOGIAL ISSUES

A New View of the Church?

One of the most significant aspects of liberation theology is its connection with the growth of "base communities"—called CEBs in Latin America, "Comunidades eclesiastico de base." In Latin America the experience of social marginalization and political powerlessness has led Christians to form small support and study groups. Starting in the 1950s as "Bible Circles" or groups of Christian labor unionists, this popular movement has come to play a major role in the development of liberation theology, especially in its later period. Perhaps they reflected the failure of the hierarchical Catholic Church and its perceived foreignness. Samuel Escobar believes they may have been modeled after Protestant small groups that were so widely (and successfully) used in evangelism during this time (1987A:26–27). Led by "Delegates of the Word," quasi-priests who had minimal training, the groups were at times ecumenical in character. As Guillermo Cook notes, "Christian commitment in crisis situations is what drives them, and not a political program" (1987:14). Accordingly, there was a strong emphasis on the study of Scripture, usually coupled with a critical social analysis (though the degree of political awareness varied—from a relative disinterest in Chile to a high degree of involvement in places like Nicaragua during the late 1970s. Escobar, 1987A:29).

Interestingly, it was during the second phase of liberation theology, during the late 1970s, that more theological significance was given to the movement. True, the stage had been set by the discussions of Vatican II on the church. There, in the dogmatic constitution *Lumen Gentium*, the church was clearly defined as the "People of God." These are said to be aided by the officers of the church, who represent Christ, preach the Gospel, and serve as stewards of the Eucharist (Flannery, ed. 1975:372, 379, 381). This language appeared to many to imply that the hierarchy was supportive of growth and outreach rather than constitutive of the nature of the church.

In Latin America these ideas were picked up in reference to the CEBs during the Puebla Conference in 1979. The bishops there noted: "This view of the Church as an historical socially structured people must also serve as the point of reference for theological reflection on the CEBs existing on our continent." Their life is to be inscribed in the context of the church as an *historical institutional people* (*Puebla Documents*, par. 261,2, quoted in Escobar, 1987A:31, his emphasis).

Jesuit J. B. Libanio has outlined the theological challenge facing the CEBs. Theology must show, in the light of the unique connection in the communities between faith and life, and between the Word of God and social commitment, that "such a unity is the Christian way of living out the faith and is the logical consequence of the correct understanding of the mystery of the incarnation" (1987:44). However, the Christians must do this, he adds, without losing their theological identity or falling prey to political manipulation—not always an easy thing in the politically charged atmosphere of Latin America.

This discussion and the events giving rise to it place us squarely in the middle of major theological tensions: How is God's role in history assessed? What is the role of the church in this? How is theological truth discerned as one is involved in social realities?

These issues have been most strikingly addressed by Leonardo Boff in his book *Ecclesiogenesis: The Base Communities Reinvent the Church* (Portuguese ed. 1977; ET 1986). Does this movement represent, he wonders, "a new type of institutional presence of Christianity in the world?" (2). A more important question is the response of the traditional churches: Will the Catholic Church discover its meaning and responsibility in the nurture of these communities or will it turn away in fear and opt for security?

These questions have been forced by the worldwide renewal movement that has spawned communities of lively faith and innovative worship within the church. Since faith in Christ constitutes communion with the body of Christ, Boff points out, "believers by reason of their faith and community are already, in themselves, the presence of the universal church" (19).

But can this popular movement be reconciled with the hierarchical structure of the church? Boff argues that this traditional function, though essential, does not subsist in and of itself; it subsists with the faith community to purify and prolong the already existing church (25). Here Boff seems to echo the statement regarding the role of the "offices" in *Lumen Gentium*: "The holders of office, who are invested with a sacred power, are, in fact, dedicated to promoting the interests of their brethren" so that the people of God will finally attain to salvation (Flannery, ed., 1975:369).

References to power and interest are, of course, sensitive issues in Latin America, but they have also surfaced in recent evangelical discussions of the church and its ministry. Are the gifts given for the preservation of the structure or for building up the living body of believers? Boff, making use of recent New Testament scholarship, is insistent that the twelve apostles were not "founders"; they were an eschatological community announcing the kingdom (50). Gifts function in persons as a manifestation of the Spirit in the community to further the kingdom (27–28).

Which is primary, he asks, the hierarchy or the people of God? He implies that the former has traditionally been the "first act," so that the laity has been marginalized and without power. But in spite of the alarming shortage of priests in Latin America, the reaction of the clergy to lay participation in worship has been fear. Why should the layperson, Boff asks, "who presides, who exercises a real ministry and a true diakonia, not be able to posit the sacramental signs of the obvious de-facto presence of Christ?" (62). The sacraments belong to the faith community by their very nature, they are not given as gifts from the outside (63–71).

Obviously we are in the midst of wrenching and far-reaching discussions on the nature of the church, with worldwide implications. But notice that these are issues that the church in Latin America is in a unique position to consider. Do inherited structures enable the people of God to fulfill their ministry, or do they hinder this ministry? Do they, in other words, empower people to serve God? That these questions threaten the holders of church power is clear from the reaction in Rome's *Instruction on Liberation Theology*:

> Building on such a conception of the Church of the People, a critique of the very structures of the Church is developed [by liberation theology]. It is not simply the case of fraternal correction of the Church whose behavior does not reflect the evangelical spirit of service and is linked to old-fashioned signs of authority which scandalize the poor. It has to do with a challenge to the *sacramental and hierarchical structure* of the Church which was willed by the Lord himself. (Ratzinger, 1984:24, his emphasis)

But the thousands of small groups meeting across the continent continue their growth in spite of such pronouncements. To those living in situations of hopelessness, studying the Bible together and praying have brought new hope. As a result, new authority patterns are developing and the whole community is being seen as a priestly community (1 Peter 2:9). This cannot help but provide us with fresh readings of Scripture and new forms of evangelism. Guillermo Cook points out that Latin America awaits a reformation. Ironically it just might be, he believes, that in the uncounted Catholic base communites—rather than in the Protestant churches—we are seeing the beginning of a such a reformation, from the bottom up (1987:20). Are these groups becoming heirs of the rich evangelical heritage of Latin America?

But this discussion leaves theological questions that must be faced. Does reference to the poor and the people tempt us to place in these communities the theological center of gravity? Are these becoming originators of God's Word rather than building themselves on the written word? Boff speaks of

102

"sacramental density" that increases from honest atheists, through anonymous Christians, to the conscious sacramental presence of Christ (7). Pablo Richard, in his discussion of the church of the poor, asks where the Word of God is truly to be found: "The biblical text is not a direct revelation of God; the text is an instrument for discernment of God's Living Word in our present-day history." And this is not merely a commentary on the Bible but "the experience of God in the history of the oppressed" (1985:32–33).

This makes us wonder whether, theologically, "the people of God" or even "the sacramental community" are adequate definitions of the church. John Calvin, for example, insists that the church exists where the Word of God is preached and heard and where the sacraments are rightly administered (*Institutes*, IV,i). When God's Word is not honored as having the special place in God's calling, the locus of authority can easily shift to those who meet in his name. Liberationists agree that God's people are formed by God himself, but they want to caution us against separating this call from his (and our own) involvement in history. This is an important claim, and it calls for response. Before responding, however, we must examine liberation theology's new way of understanding spirituality and God's presence in history.

A New Spirituality?

An early criticism of liberation theology, which we have noted, was that it did nothing for the spiritual life of people or for the renewal of the church. In some ways the rise of the base-community movement has blunted this criticism. But the activism of liberation theology leaves people wondering whether spirituality, at least the way most people think of it, has any role to play. In recent years important discussions have turned this criticism into a forum for suggesting a wholly new way of relating to God (see especially Eduardo Bonnin, ed., 1982).

Traditionally spiritual life and devotional practices have been associated with special times and places: Sundays and feast days, churches and monasteries. Liberation theologians, speaking from their place of commitment to the poor, argue that this conception of spirituality is limited. It suggests that God is to be found by retreating from the world and its tensions, that true spirituality is resting in the peace of his presence. It is clear that liberation theology believes this is a limited view of how God is experienced. They want to ask: How will God be known by the marginalized and powerless? Since, as we have seen, the God of Scripture is involved with the poor and suffering, and his ear is open to their cry, they will surely experience him as an ally in their struggles to find dignity and liberation. If this is so, we must not retreat from these struggles to find God; rather, we must seek them out. "The commitment to liberation for the Christian ought to be the place of encounter with God and therefore the primary source of spirituality" (ibid.:12, 13).

What are we to make of this claim? It seems that some liberation theologians say we are to take it literally: the experience of God is to be found primarily in the political practice of liberation. Pablo Richard, for example, asserts, "The origin of all evangelization is the *experience of God* in the history of the oppressed.... This spirituality is not reduced to the level of individual sentiment, but rather finds its corporate and communal expression in any number of ways: celebrations, songs and prayers" (Richard, 1985:31, his emphasis). This implies that the experience of God takes place as we encounter him in the practice of liberation, and this experience is only then celebrated in songs and prayers. We know him as we work together on the common project of liberation.

This is not to say that we do not take time out from our work to call on God. But this period of time does not take us out of the world at all; rather it relates us more specifically to God and what he is doing in the world, "since it consists in lending a more attentive ear to his word that is transmitted by what happens in time ... this activity of reflection and interpretation is prayer" (Segundo, 1974:44–45). For Segundo all of this is to the end that we follow Jesus more closely.

Prayer must be situated within this larger discipleship, which he defines as the "Christian project . . . the fashioning of love in history; or . . . the liberation of the universe from all the enslavements that weigh down upon it" (ibid).

In a more recent discussion *We Drink From Our Own Wells* (1984), Gustavo Gutiérrez puts a slightly different coloring on spirituality: our commitment to Christ accompanies, and seems to lead, our commitment to our neighbors. The context of Latin America, he reminds us, is experienced as one of death-dealing. Our age is one in which the poor are experiencing new hope in their struggles, a new sense of God's presence. We must learn to drink from their wells. Experiencing life and seeing God from their point of view, Gutiérrez believes, would provide a breakthrough and a new integration in the classic tension between contemplation and action (1984:18–20).

How are we to understand this integration? Spirituality, Gutiérrez argues, is always embodied; it is a particular way of being Christian. For Gutiérrez this means to live in and with the struggles of the Latin American poor who call out to God, to call out to God with them and feel the power of God on their behalf. In this community we experience life in the spirit as a power that dwells in the deepest part of us and confronts the alienation we feel around us (60, 64). Here Jesus is our model. He lived in his task of proclaiming the Gospel; that was where his Father's business was located: "to pitch camp in the midst of human history and there give witness to the Father's love" (41).

If my reading of this is accurate, it seems that Gutiérrez is marking an important shift in discussions of liberation spirituality. Genuine life with God is found, he seems to say, not primarily in the practice of liberation but in the commitment to Christ that issues in that practice. Both the commitment and the practice are "first acts"—we both contemplate and practice who God is. Only afterwards do we think about him. First come silence, mysticism, and commitment, and only later comes respectful discourse about him. "To do theology without mediation of both contemplation and practice is tantamount to being outside the demands of the God of the Bible" (Gutiérrez quoted in R. Allen Hatch, 1985:10; see also S. Galilea in Bonnin, ed., 1982:35–38).

Rather than making spirituality dependent on liberation method, Gutiérrez seems to want to do the reverse: to make his method into a process of spirituality (1984:136). This is spelled out further in the final section of this book. Following Jesus becomes a continuing conversion and a break with sin (involving social analysis, uncovering unjust mechanisms), then pardon and openness to new possibilities. In the midst of death the experience of Christ's resurrection gives new meaning; in dark nights one meets the Lord (ibid., 131).

Is this a new starting point for theological reflection in which commitment to Christ replaces (or leads) our political commitment to liberation? Or is this merely another way of describing our precommitment to liberation? If it is the former, then the community of faith may become a new locus for reflecting on Scripture, for seeing and experiencing God before we actually reflect on him. As René Padilla puts this, "The gathered community of believers is meant to be the organ through which the Word of God takes up a fresh meaning in relation to a concrete historical situation" (1983:81).

But can even this commitment really be a "first act"? Is this not a response, however inchoate, to hearing the challenge and promises of God in the Gospel? Perhaps, though, Gutiérrez is helping us see that our method is a circle of spiritual growth—from hearing the word, through response and commitment (to God and our neighbor), to reflection and further obedience. Christine Gudorf points out that in the early church, metaphysics developed out of spirituality (1987:15); perhaps this is happening today in Latin America as well.

In spite of the ambiguities that remain, it is hard to overemphasize the importance of this struggle to articulate a "worldly" spirituality. In the North our greatest weakness is a spiritual poverty in the face of the incessant demands of modern life. The traditional spirituality that encourages only retreat and quiet has left us feeling vaguely guilty. Liberation theology encourages us to think of our experience with God as constituted in the midst of life, not on its edges, and to see prayer and Bible reading as directed to a concrete realization of the kingdom in the actual struggle for righteousness and peace, especially on behalf of the powerless. Liberation theology may here be providing a much needed encouragement toward develping a vital lay spirituality.

God and History: How Are They Related?

Discussions of the nature of the church and of the Christian life will always lead to the fundamental issue of how God is related to this world. In Latin America this question has taken on a particular urgency. To people struggling to make a life for themselves, traditional concepts of God couched in abstract and static categories have seemed, not only irrelevant, but an actual betrayal of the biblical picture of God. As a result, liberation theology has carried on a sustained and sometimes bitter polemic against theology that pictures God as distant and uninvolved. There are not two worlds—God's world and this world—but "one God-filled history" (Miguez Bonino, 1975:137). And it is here in this world that God is manifest and known.

Western theologians have predictably responded to this line of argument with alarm. And at first glance, in this approach there does appear to be an implicit categorical mistake. While it may be true that God cannot be *known* outside of our experience and obedience, it does not follow that he does not *exist* beyond this experience. But the issue cannot be disposed of quite as simply as this. For whatever the facts of God's existence, we have no independent access to him apart from our historical interaction with him and with his truth revealed in Scripture. Even Scripture did not come to us "out of heaven," so to speak, but was mediated through the historical events and personages of the biblical period. So it seems hard to deny Miguez' point that "there seems to be in the Bible no relation of man to himself, to his neighbor, or even to God which is not mediated in terms of man's *work*" (ibid., 109, his emphasis).

Surely closer attention to this fact will have an impact on the way we think about God. Juan Luis Segundo believes it will transform our thinking. For unlike our theology manuals, the New Testament does not deal with God at all in his eternity. "It is here in this 'now' in the 'historical' end-result, so to speak, that the three names appear and their being is revealed" (1974:21). God comes to us only in and through history. This fact is summed up, Segundo argues, in the biblical teaching on the covenant. God makes himself known as "person" and as "freedom" (important categories of our theology) only in and through his dealings with Abraham, Isaac, and Jacob—through his interaction with human persons (ibid., 23).

Similarly we cannot know God outside of our involvement with this dramatic exchange, climaxing in the coming of Christ. Before Christ, Segundo believes, God had avoided identifying himself with any and every human project, but with Christ's coming "our history invades the divine realm" (27). Before Christ, God appeared in salvation history; after Christ, God is interested in the salvation of history. Into this world the Spirit has been sent, "attuned to the rhythm of history" (29). So God himself is revealed to us only in terms of this history: "God opened up the mystery of this being to us in order to show us a total and intimate collaboration in a history of love that is our own history" (63). This dynamic and inescapable presence of God, since the Incarnation, has led liberation theology to insist on the social as well as the personal dimension of sin. That is, sin is not only a personal (and inward) rebellion against God; it is also a refusal to collaborate with God in his liberating work. It is not only a matter of rebelling in our hearts but also of cheating in the streets and offices. In fact, Segundo defines the sin against the Holy Spirit as "precisely the refusal to accompany Jesus in his work of liberation" (45).

Again we see the close interrelation between our practice—that is, our obedience—and our understanding of God. This leads to a novel interpretation of John 17:12—"I have many things to say to you but you cannot bear them now."

This means, Segundo argues, that "the world would have to undergo a transformation for you to be able to understand many aspects of this truth, this truth which I am" (29). Our experience of collaboration with God's work "will be the best foundation for the further purification of our notion of God" (69).

Before we conclude that God is here being held captive to certain (previously made) political and social choices, Segundo and his colleagues would remind us that, in the West, God has often been held captive to social and political choices we have made. Because for us the ideal of personhood is the free and fulfilled individual, God has become the free and transcendent person par excellence, the One who calls us to individual fulfillment. Can we not allow people living in a corporate and unceasing struggle to free themselves from oppression to see God as the One coming alongside to deliver them? Indeed, is one image any more biblical than the other?

Moreover, liberation theology reminds us, in our Western tradition, knowledge of God was mediated by the Holy Spirit usually in terms of what we call "communion"—his Spirit bearing witness with ours (Rom. 8:16). Now is it not possible that the knowledge of God can also be mediated through the practice of discipleship (1 John 3:10), just as knowledge of other persons is mediated both by communion (of which the supreme experience is termed the "act" of love) and by working on common projects?

This analogy provides a helpful reminder of how we come to know each other, but it suggests a caution as well. For just as the other person always transcends and remains free over the work we do together, so does God's person transcend that work. Did God identify himself as completely with this historical project as Segundo and others would have us believe? Is it not going too far to say with Segundo, "Now everything is under man's dominion. And above man there is only Christ: that is the whole Christ, the Christ who is affected by what happens in each of his brothers, the Christ who recapitulates all humanity. It is there that we encounter God" (74)? What place does this leave for that final (and surprising!)

consummation, when God will do things that no eye has yet seen nor ear heard?

We return, then, to the central tension that liberation theology leaves with us. We saw it in the dicussion of the church: How does the presence of Christ with his people relate to his sovereignly given gifts? And we have seen it in spirituality: How does our encounter with him in this world anticipate the promised fulfillment of face-to-face knowledge? And we see it here: Does God's revelation of himself in history hold nothing in reserve? Here it seems to me that it is not the special context of Latin America that has caused problems so much as liberation theology's dependence on particular Western influences. For the hand of Teilhard de Chardin is heavy on the writings of Segundo, especially in the former's emphasis on the christification of history. And in liberation theology in general the influence of Karl Rahner is often to be seen, especially in the emphasis on the dynamic unity between world history and salvation history and the significance of the teleological orientation of the people to communion with God (see discussion of these things in F. P. Fiorenza, 1974:456–57).

The irony is how often these same influences have been used elsewhere to support reformist politics. In contrast to this evolutionary schema, the evangelical call to radical commitment and transformation has sounded in Latin America as a clarion call, already in the nineteenth century. It was a call "to change, to transformation, centered in the religious sphere, but with repercussions in the totality of life and of society" (Miguez in Richard, ed., 1985:243). This seems a better focus than Segundo's plea that everything religious must be translated into "man's tasks in history" (78). True, Segundo wants in the end to allow for transcendence. The laity, he argues, after they have seen their work as creative, may again be able to attribute real value to "the trancendental aspect of the message" (176), because one cannot lay hold of God by starting from the history of people! (175). Perhaps in liberation theology more should be made of this theological priority. For after our stumbling and imperfect obedience, we discover that it was God who, in the beginning, had laid hold of us. Here perhaps we have the real "first act."

WHAT HAVE WE LEARNED FROM LIBERATION THEOLOGY?

A New Role for the Social Sciences

A major contribution of liberation theology has been the introduction and use of the social sciences as a means of better comprehending the setting in which theology is done. Making use of some of the recent insights in the sociology of knowledge, liberation theology has reminded us that there is no knowledge that is not shaped by the social situation of the knower. A corollary of this, now commonly accepted, even by critics of liberation theology, is that all readings of Scripture will reflect to a certain degree the point of view of the interpreter.

A further, and more controversial, application of this principle involves the political commitments of the interpreter. Liberation theology insists that interpreters who read Scripture from the point of view of privilege tend to be blind to issues of power and oppression, whereas those who read it from the point of view of the powerless are drawn to the way God sides with the weak and to the fact that Jesus' message is often summarized as good news to the poor. This is a major insight that has implications not only for hermeneutics but also for theology. For how would salvation be defined by one who tended to overlook issues of power and oppression? As is clear from many discussions of salvation in the West, issues of personal and emotional security and fulfillment come naturally to the fore. But what would a person see who reads the same text from the point of view of the marginalized? Obviously this person would be led to define salvation in terms of actual experiences of power and deliverance, often with important political implications. He or she would agree with South African liberationist Manas Buthelezei who insists, "Any discussion about the humanization of life which excludes the dynamics of power is a fruitless theoretical exercise" (in Torres and Fabella, eds., 1978:85).

An equally important contribution of liberation theology's use of social science is the challenge these theologians have mounted to the received structural/functionalist model of society and to the reigning developmental paradigm. After the 1980s, it is harder than ever to have confidence in models of economic growth that do not deal with structural issues of dependency. Take, for example, UNESCO director J. P. Grant's description of the plight of children in Latin America. Twenty-five million children in Latin America are inadequately fed, he points out, even though this region has become, after the United States, the world's major food exporter. What is the problem? No degree of technical advance, he insists, can solve the inequities that exist in that region. Only "the reversal of today's financial flows in favor of the developing world—via debt reduction, trade agreements and increased aid—would stimulate demand and create jobs" (*The State of the World's Children.* 1989:25). Because the debt crisis brings with it increasing poverty, especially of women and children, Andrew Kirk's assessment seems truer than ever: "It is difficult to deny that the interpretive tool of 'dependence' most adquately describes the economic situation of the underdeveloped countries in the Third World today" (1980:128).

This recognition, however, needs to be placed in perspective. No model can capture every dimension of a complex problem. Thus, while the dependency model will illuminate areas to which we (especially in the North) have previously been blind, the functionalist model may still help to supplement these insights. It may, for example, do more to help us see what traditional or cultural blocks to development might exist, or what traditional resources might be available to create self-reliance. The fact that liberation economists are not yet ready to concede such an interaction of models may indicate a blind spot of their own.

Finally, the use of the social sciences has alerted us all to the role that practice (or, in biblical terms, obedience) will inevitably play in a growing understanding of Scripture. This has helped many observers to become aware of the way abstract formulations have sometimes actually impeded obedience in Western theology. A clear example of this is a fiction that people in the West have tended to hold—that one can approach Scripture from a politically neutral point of view. The truth is, of course, that our political commitments are largely hidden from our consciousness but that they are nevertheless a part of the presuppositions we bring to the text. Usually in the North such neutrality can go unnoticed, but in a situation where one is confronted with urgent choices with life-and-death consequences, such a fiction can actually impede obedience.

Liberation theology has encouraged us to see this interplay between understanding and practice in terms of a dialectic (some prefer to say a "spiral"), in which our understanding grows as we respond to God's Word in appropriate ways. Many people now wonder how it is possible to understand the actual process of biblical interpretation in any other way.

But Does Philosophy Have No Role to Play?

This use of social science has given us tools for the theological task that have proven extremely useful. But as with any advance, the progress has come at a certain cost. We have noticed that the major liberationist thinkers have proclaimed that the social sciences have replaced philosophy as an interpretive tool for doing theology. Traditionally philosophy has been the handmaiden of theology. This has led, so it is believed by liberation theologians, to an understanding of theology as rationality. Now we see that practice must play a greater (even a leading) role in the process of knowing God. Accordingly, we must use those sciences that deal with practice, the social and political sciences. And so the role previously played by philosophy is now played by these newer disciplines.

This reading of theological method, it seems to me, contains a serious oversimplification. Indeed, it could be argued that the major weaknesses in liberation theology stem from this single confusion. Social science and philosophy cannot be interchanged in this way, for they do not fulfill the same function. It is true that philosophy as traditionally conceived provided a conceptual framework within which theology could be carried out. And this process was thought to happen without much interaction with social and political realities. But, at least since Immanuel Kant, philosophy has come to provide not only an ideological framework but also, and more importantly, critical tools for evaluating such frameworks. Sociological location has certainly become one of the factors in this critical analysis, but this can only show the source of the influences on our thinking, it cannot judge their truth or falsity.

The irony here is that liberation theology has dismissed philosophy from its methodology at the very moment it has put on the table issues with deep philosophical implications. We have already observed that liberation theology has helped us see the close relation between theory and practice, but at the same time any sophisticated discussion of this relationship has been missing. Outside of vague remarks about how love maintains a sense of transcendence (Miguez Bonino 1983:113) or an assurance that we cannot get to the living God by starting with the human situation (Segundo, 1974:175), we are given little help in knowing how theory and practice relate.

This weakness is pointed out (and illustrated!) in Clodovis Boff's major discussion *Theology and Praxis* (ET 1987). This is the most ambitious attempt to sketch a methodology in which praxis is given a legitimate role. Boff readily acknowledges what everybody knows: while there has much sloganeering in liberation theology, a well-thought-out method has not been forthcoming (1987:xxii). Yet his own attempt at what he calls an "epistemological recasting" is mired—a further irony—in the European intellectualist tradition that liberation theology has tried so heroically to escape (interestingly the book was his doctoral dissertation at Louvain, the Catholic university of Belgium!).

Much of his argument will be applauded in traditional circles. He argues helpfully for the primacy of theology over practice. Evangelicals will appreciate his concern not to allow theology to be taken captive by alien ideologies (of which the most dangerous is Marxism). Too many studies of liberation theology, he points out, have no "discriminating relationship to the word of God that founds [Christian] theology, and hence cannot be taken for constitutively theological analysis" (69). Such a statement from a central figue in liberation theology is as welcome as it is surprising.

But what role, then, does praxis play in theology? It is certainly not, he claims, the criterion of truth, for practice represents what is to be explained, not what explains (200). But praxis can fire theory, get it going, on the one hand (188), and can be applied to history on the other: "Theological truth can be practiced in history and political practice can be a true practice" (19).

So he argues for the primacy of theory over practice, a step we can appreciate. But he goes beyond this to argue for the purity of theory from the influence of practice. Theology, we are told, is autonomous as theoretical truth (16); when reflecting its proper object (God and his Word), it is knowledge structured in a discourse. Anything is pertinent theologically only when considered under a certain rational form (71–74). Praxis, then, while necessary to faith, cannot be pertinent to theology. In the end theory and practice, theology and faith, represent irreducible orders: they call for each other and interact, but they are totally separate (he uses the Chalcedonian formula "without mixture or confusion," 214). There is, he insists, no necessary correlation between theology and holiness (201).

One wants to ask Boff how theory and practice can be bound up with each other if their relations are merely external, if in the end they cannot influence one another. It appears that just at the point where liberation theology bodes well to make its most original contribution—the epistemological significance of Christian practice—Boff has retreated to the strict dichotomy (between knowledge and reality, doing and knowing) of European rationalism. Is this not another form of the theory/application model of knowing that liberation thinkers (especially Freire) have rejected?

The primacy of theory over practice must certainly be preserved. Christianity, for example, insists that the fundamental problem with human society is that sin has caused a break between God and humanity. This is a necessary part of the "theory" that is implicit in our analysis of society. As a result, this analysis must investigate religious factors that might reflect this fundamental estrangement. Now while it is true that our analysis and practice will illumine the form that this abnormality takes in society—our theory will be modified by practice, as we will argue momentarily—the theory is at least logically, if not always temporally, prior to our practice. Since theology is bound to the world-changing self-revelation of God, culminating in Christ, it must maintain the ultimate primacy of theory (see the discussion in Volf, 1983:17). Even if the meaning of this is clear only as we obey God's Word, we approach society with the assumption, as the *Instruction* from Rome puts it, that "liberation is first and foremost liberation from the radical slavery of sin" (1984:3).

But it seems impossible to argue, as Boff does, that our theory is pure of any influence of praxis. We have noted that liberation theology has sometimes given practice, or the pretheoretical commitment to liberation, a privileged position—as though it were pure of any influence of theory. But as Andrew Kirk points out, "In fact no theology is able to reflect on pristine practice; all practice is already the result of some kind of ideological and cultural conditioning" (1980:128). Here it seems that liberation theology has not followed its own advice of subjecting all practice to analysis in order to determine whose interest it serves.

But just as there can be no "pure practice," neither can there be "pure theory," theory that is not influenced by a set practices. Liberation theology has consistently insisted (Boff's arguments are an exception) that there is no autonomous knowledge, that all knowledge is embodied in social practice. Accordingly, truth can be fully discovered only as we are involved in the practice of that truth. Surely the result of an action is one of the ways of measuring its truth, but it is not the only way of doing so, as some liberationists argue (Boff is on target here: to call praxis the criterion of truth empties it of rationality and leaves us with a voluntaristic epistemology [196]). Put another way, while we may allow a pragmatic test for truth, this does not constitute an adequate theory of truth. For praxis is not privileged, nor is it ideologically neutral. In determining truth, just as in interpreting Scripture, theory and practice must have a reciprocal relationship.

As I argued in the introduction, our knowledge of Scripture is of primary importance in living the Christian life, it is constitutive of our theory; but this is not a disembodied knowledge. Our understanding of Scripture is conditioned by our environment and shaped by our obedience. This conditioning not only provides the impetus for understanding but also influences the form that our insight takes. Practice, then, inevitably has epistemological significance. According to the New Testament, knowledge grows out of obedience (e.g., John 7:17). What we see there might justly be called an epistemology of obedience.

A final irony of these discussions lies in the fact that just as liberation theology has broached these enormously important issues, it has chosen to ignore those (primarily Anglo-American) philosophical conversations that have formed a new appreciation for the role of action in the process of knowing. In all the liberationist treatments of theory and practice that I have read, I have seen no reference to the pragmatic and empirical traditions that stem from Charles Pierce in America and John Stuart Mill in Britain. I have referred previously to the work of Charles Taylor, who has learned from this tradition, but I could add thinkers like Michael Polanyi and evangelical Jerry Gill.

Polanyi has argued, for example, that "knowing [is] an active comprehension of the things known, action that requires skill" (1958:vii). And Gill defends the notion that some things cannot be known at all apart from our responding to them in appropriate ways (1971). The critical tools these thinkers are developing are specifically designed to help us make use of the findings of social science in a self-critical way. The failure of liberation theology to develop any philosophical sophistication may account for its lack of critical rigor in its interaction with the social sciences in general and with Marxism in particular.

The Contribution of Liberation Theology

After saying all this, I must quickly acknowledge that such philosophical failings are not unique to liberation theology. Theologians of every place and time have had their ideological blindspots. In fact one could argue that the weaknesses of liberation theology reflect a larger and longer standing failure in Christianity as a whole. It is safe to say that in the whole of its history, the church has come to no explicit consensus of how biblical truth relates to social and political issues. Being the religion of the rulers for most of its history, Christianity has too often been able to avoid direct encounters with these issues (all the while, liberation theology points out, embodying a particular, Constantinian political framework).

But in our century the inequities of modernization and two world wars have made these issues inescapable. At the beginning of the 1900s the social gospel movement sought to develop a social theology that would address problems created by an overly rapid urbanization. Like all pioneering movements, its zeal led it to excesses, as the fundamentalists were quick to point out. But fundamentalism, for its part, being largely reactionary in character, had no positive and constructive way of dealing with these same social problems.

Now liberation theology, in many ways in the tradition of the social gospel movement, has seized the initiative and sought to confront massive injustice. Its leaders have forced us to confront the challenge that we have long avoided: Will the church face up to the immense social and political tensions of the developing world? As might be expected, evangelicals have often dismissed this movement as a newer form of the social gospel. But as Samuel Escobar and his colleagues have pointed out, squeezing this debate into the older liberal/fundamentalist categories, as missionaries have tended to do, is not helpful (Escobar et al., 1983:54). Moreover, the conservative claim that by changing individuals one can change society, whatever its validity in the North, may not apply in the communal orientation of Latin America. Studies of conservative groups in Latin America show that a change in the individual has not brought about social change (see Sidney Rooy, 1986:76).

The issues that liberation theology wrestles with are not going away; if anything, they are growing more insistent. It seems to me the very fact that evangelicals in Latin America, especially since 1985, have become so polarized over liberation theology is itself evidence that these issues are now an inevitable fact of Christian life in Latin America and they must be faced. Rather than dismissing liberation theology as an aberration within Christianity, we must learn from it, even from its mistakes, but above all we must build on its advances. The challenge of René Padilla seems unavoidable:

> We can reject the philosophical premises of the movement. We can object to many of their theological statements. . . . Nevertheless, are we going to ignore the legitimacy of the . . . project as an effort to deal with the situation of the Latin American people and to "theologize" starting from their situation? The only theology that the Bible knows is a "functional" theology, that is to say, a theology in dialogue with the concrete reality, a theology at the service of praxis. The only way to live an authentic Christian life is to take seriously Jesus Christ's incarnation. Here lies the greatest challenge [of liberation theology]: in its call to reflect in the context of a concrete engagement and make theology an instrument of transformation (quoted in Torres and Fabella, eds, 1978:213).

While evangelicals have become polarized, I have been impressed with the humility that major theologians of the movement have shown in recent years. Miguez Bonino admitted in 1985 that "the contribution of the Church is basically in the area of defining and introducing values and not in the formulation of ideologies and the creation of institutions" (in Richard, ed., 1985:249). In his address to the American

Academy of Religion in New York, from which I have quoted, Gustavo Gutiérrez admitted that liberation thinkers have made mistakes and have not always been properly understood. "After 16 years I think Liberation Theology's emphases are not new but very traditional (I used to think they were new). Perhaps our work is to remind us of old things again" (public lecture, AAR, 9 December 1984).

Samuel Escobar concludes his book with a summary of some of these "old things," and his listing may help us see ways we can profit from an interaction with liberation theology (see 1987:170–82). He reminds us that the God who liberated his people from Egypt is still a liberating God today. Although we must interpret the Exodus in terms of Christ, we must not spiritualize it altogether: God is still the God of justice. Moreover, we need to understand Christ today in terms of an imitation of his historicial life and lifestyle. Jesus, who in his missionary style identified with the workers and proclaimed the Gospel as good news to the poor, calls us to similar concrete commitments. Do our comfortable situations impede us from feeling the depths of this challenge? Do they keep us from hearing the cries of people like Carolina Maria de Jesus with whose story I began this chapter? Escobar concludes his summary by saying that it would be tragic if out of fear of liberation theology we would lose the great heritage of the Gospel and its power to transform and simply continue a conservative support for oppression. These are indeed old challenges, but they are new as well, like the new commandment that Jesus left us. As the apostle John explains this, "If anyone has material possessions and sees his brother in need but has no pity on him, how can the love of God be in him? Dear children, let us not love with words or tongue but with actions and in truth" (1 John 3:17–18).

4

ASIAN THEOLOGY: CHRISTIANITY AND THE TRANSCENDENT

Flower on a rainy night
Flower on a rainy night
Fell on the ground in the wind and rain
It sighs day and night
It has fallen not to rise again.

Rain-drops, rain-drops
You lead us into the pool of suffering
Not mindful of our frailty
Covering our destiny with darkness
Causing us to fall from the branch
Out of everyone's sight.
　　　　(Taiwanese Folksong, Trans. by C. S. Song)

THE ASIAN CONTEXT

Asia is a varied spiritual and religious universe set amid a mosaic of affluence and poverty. The presence of Christianity is small—2 or 3 percent in most places; only in Indonesia (10–12 percent) and the Philippines (85 percent) are numbers significant—though its influence has been greater than these figures imply. But from the beginning it has had to face stronger (and prouder!) cultural and religious traditions than anywhere else in the world. While Asia features a greater diversity than either of our other two regions, there is a unity given by the presence and vigor of major religious traditions—Hinduism, Buddhism, Taoism, and, to a lesser extent, Islam. These traditions have given their cultures a deeply philosophical and religious—the two cannot be separated in Asia—worldview. The solidity of these traditions was such that even the onslaught of colonialism and neocolonialism has not been able to diminish their role. Indians, even of the lowest castes, pity foreigners who are not able to advance through the stages of karma to eventual Nirvana. Chinese, who think of their country as the "middle kingdom" of the earth, are so confident of their nobility that they are famous for their fear and suspicion of outsiders. Missionaries to Asia found a people so proud of their past that they were usually incredulous as to why they should give up this noble heritage for a foreign faith.

The Religious Context

What is the nature and attraction of this heritage? One must bear in mind the incredible diversity of schools and views that have developed during the three thousand years of history in widely diverse cultures. Still at the risk of oversimplification we may take the basic world picture of Hinduism as typical—especially as this is embodied in the Hindu Scriptures, the Upanishads and the Bhagavad Gita, both composed before the coming of Christ. These portray the Brahman as the ultimate spiritual unity pervading all things: "Verily in the beginning, this word was Brahman" (Upanishads, Maitri). This ultimate reality is evolving itself as this world, the shining spirit through whose light all this shines (Katha II.2.15). All that exists expresses and is grounded in this one indestructible reality (See Baird and Bloom, 1971).

From the subjective point of view this spirit is experienced as Atman, or the self, which is immediately felt and known. This "self," when conceived separately, is really a product of ignorance, but it is the means by which we perceive the absolute. The true self is experienced in mystical unity with the Brahman, an event that cannot be described but only immediately and intuitively known.

But our ordinary experience in the world is a barrier to this awareness of unity. For in our ignorance we experience it as solid and real, when in fact it is really an illusion, or maya. This idea was especially developed by Sankara (d. 820 A.D.), though it was present earlier, especially in the Gita. Sometimes truth is presented in such a dazzling way that our minds do not grasp the inner reality it expresses. To reach Brahman, we must shake off these delusions, an experience called moksha or release, so that we can reach the state of complete oneness with Brahman, or Nirvana. This has led to the typical Asian identification of spirituality with renunciation of the world.

This process of salvation involves a gradual development through many incarnations. The basic law of this process is called karma, a kind of cosmic cause and effect. The Gita makes it clear that no embodied being can completely re-nounce action (18:11). Indeed the universe itself depends on actions; so in a sense our work keeps up the cycle of the universe. We perform it, however, in a detached spirit, for desire or interest would imply bondage to maya. All these actions have effects and consequences that determine the future. These laws are inviolable; thus a lower caste person does not fight his or her karma, but rather seeks to live in harmony with it.

Buddhism, which may be described as a renewal move-ment within Hinduism, derives from the teaching of Siddhar-tha Gautama Buddha (563–481 B.C.). Following his enlighten-ment, he taught the four noble truths. The first is the recognition that the essence of life in the world is suffering. Our existence is marked by three things: impermanence (*anicca*), nonsubstance (*anatta*) and suffering (*dukkha*). Sec-ond, the basic cause of suffering is desire based on ignorance of true reality. But, third, there is release from this bondage to desire and suffering. This way of escape is described in the fourth truth: the eightfold path to enlightenment (right-mind-edness, action, speech, concentration, etc.). Notice this philo-sophical analysis of the human situation is at the same time the path to religious enlightenment. In Asia religion and philosophy are always integrated (see the discussion of D. Lim in Samuel and Sugden, 1983).

Hinduism and Buddhism have proven extremely hardy

and resilient faiths, appearing in many schools and movements across the centuries, and they have produced a people with a unique spiritual sensitivity and longing for salvation. For Africans it was the cultural malaise, for Latin Americans the economic oppression, both occasioned by Western colonialism, that provided the impetus for theological reflection. In Asia it is the religious dislocation that is the most obvious casualty of modern civilization and thus the stimulus for indigenous theology. Already early in the century violent conflicts broke out in many countries of Asia between proponents of the modern way and those of traditional values. Subsequently communist and capitalist ideologies, each in its own way, have introduced materialistic values that have eroded this Asian spirituality. Indian historian K. M. Panikkar has argued that the domination of these Western values led to "a period of social anarchy caused by the breakdown of religion and ethics, with [Asia's] intellectuals groping toward a new life" (quoted by Pfaff, 1989:6). As William Pfaff observes, "That period is still not over"—as religious riots in Tibet and democracy demonstrations in China testify (ibid.). As is the case in other Third World countries, Christianity has sometimes (e.g., in India) sided with indigenous values over against the modernizing trends, and sometimes (e.g., in China) it has been caught in the struggle between the two.

In any case this clash between deeply held religious values and the challenges of a modern secular society provides the central problem for theological discussions in Asia. The Sri Lankan theologian Aloysius Pieris has argued that a radical reappropriation of this religious tradition is a necessary part of the work of Asian theologians. Asia is unique in that the religious framework is what he calls "meta-cosmic," or oriented to transcendent communion. There are "cosmic" religions in Asia (they are sometimes called animist faiths), but, Pieris argues, they do not exist in their pure form; they are always integrated into one of the three meta-cosmic soteriologies—Hinduism, Buddhism, or Taoism (1979:32).

Pieris defines the salvific orientation of meta-cosmic faiths (including Christianity) as follows: belief in "the existence of a transphenomenal reality immanently operative in the cosmos and soteriologically available within the human person either through *agape* (redeeming love) or through *gnosis* (redeeming knowledge)" (1988:55). The challenge to Christianity in Asia, he believes, is clear. Cosmic faiths call for fulfillment in a meta-cosmic framework. Conversion to Christianity, then, is easy when cosmic faiths exist in purer form (as they did, for example, in the Philippines). But Christian reflection in Asia must begin with the understanding of the deep spiritual longing for transcendent union that exists among the people (an orientation that is threatened, Pieris argues, both by Western capitalism and Marxist materialism). Moreover, it must reckon with the fact that the religions of Asia already direct their worshipers toward this goal. In some sense then, he argues, what is called for is not the inculturation of Christianity (as in Africa) but its inreligionization (ibid., 52).

We will want to return to his argument below. Suffice it here to point out that whereas Christians in Africa are faced with cultural issues, and Latin American believers wrestle with political questions, it is the religious context of Asia and the continent-wide longing for salvation that has become the starting point for theological reflection.

Christianity in Asia

This religious sensitivity seems to have been recognized by the earliest missionaries. Matthew Ricci (1552–1610) recognized the need to meet Chinese culture at the religious and philosophical level. The first modern missionary to India, Bartholomeus Ziegenbalg, who arrived in 1706, considered the educated Brahmins ignorant until he studied the Hindu Scriptures. There he saw a small light of the Gospel and wrote in 1710 that he was amazed "how far they had come by the light of their reason in the knowledge of God and of the natural order and how by their natural powers, they often put to shame many Christians by their upright life, also showing a much greater striving for the future life" (quoted in Chandran, 1978:160).

When William Carey left Britain in 1793, Christianity was hardly known in Asia. Thanks to the work of Ziegenbalg and others, there were a few thousand Christians in India. But there were virtually none in China or Japan, and only a few in Indonesia and the Pacific Islands (Neill, 1964:153). Immediately upon their arrival, Carey and his colleagues saw that they must understand not only the "language but the thought world of these to whom the Gospel is preached" (ibid., 264). As a result, his studies of Bengali were so thorough that he is considered by the experts to be the father of Bengali prose literature (265). In spite of such respect, few missionaries before our century felt that Indian thought, or Asian thought in general, should have an impact on the way Christianity is understood (that is, on theology). Our discussion will focus on this awakening and the challenges (and dangers!) that attended it. From the many contexts of Asia, I select four that represent the major regions—India and Sri Lanka, China, Japan, and the Philippines. In each case I select, somewhat arbitrarily, a major thelogical issue to focus on that has emerged in these areas. A conclusion will attempt a general assessment of these discussions.

INDIA AND SRI LANKA AND
THE THEOLOGY OF THE PERSON

Serious rethinking of theology in India has come primarily as a result of what is called the Hindu renaissance in the nineteenth and early twentieth centuries—a movement stimulated in large measure by the challenge mounted by colonial rule and the attendant Western influence. It is interesting that the most signficant leaders of this movement (such as Ram Mohan Roy and Keshub Chandra Sen) were themselves influenced by Christian teaching (Chandran, 1978:161–162). In any case those most creative in rethinking Christianity were nourished by these revitalized traditions.

Sundar Singh (1889–1929) was born into a devout Sikh family in the Punjab (the Sikh religion is a Hindu sect that has assimilated certain elements of Islam). His devout mother read the Bhagavad Gita and told her son to ask God every morning for spiritual food before he took his breakfast (Appasamy, 1958:17). He developed a deep longing for God that his Hindu teachers could not satisfy. He continued to ask God to reveal himself to him, and in 1904 he had a luminous vision of Christ (the first of many he was to have during his life) that transformed him. Soon after, at age sixteen, he became a Christian Sadhu (teacher). This experience with Christ, much like the experience of Saul of Tarsus, had a profound influence on his thinking. From it he concluded that God was not present in everything, as his Hindu teachers claimed. Since he had practiced Yoga without satisfaction and experienced periods of deep gloom, he wondered how God could be in him. He concluded that it was the particular experience of Christ that gave him joy in the midst of suffering (ibid., 138). His life became characterized by a deep communion with God through Christ to such an extent that he longed to pass from this life to fuller communion beyond (211). For him it was the intuitive vision as opposed to discursive knowledge about God that attracted him. Indeed, on his travel in the West he often commented on the spiritual emptiness of such knowledge (231).

Sadhu Sundar Singh preached his simple message to throngs in India and the West. He died on a preaching mission to Tibet, but his impact continued on in a generation of Christian leaders. A. J. Appasamy (1891–1975), for example, met Singh while studying at Oxford in the 1920s and went on to write several major studies of the teacher's life and thought. This influence led Appasamy to find in the Bhakti tradition of Hinduism nourishment for his Christian faith, for this tradition focused one's love and adoration on a personal God, on whose mercy one can depend utterly. The quest for personal communion with God, Appasamy came to believe, was fulfilled in Christ. He was careful to reject whatever in the Bhakti teaching was inconsistent with his faith in Christ (e.g., caste, transmigration). Later he became a bishop in South India, where he promoted revivals and evangelical piety. In his understanding of his faith he believed not only that the Gospel was being reformulated but also that his own Indian heritage was being renewed (Chandran, 1978:164–65).

A missionary influential in the growing appreciation for the Indian context was Earle Stanley Jones (1884–1973), who sought to interpret Christianity as the fulfillment of India's own spiritual longings. In his 1925 book, *Christ of the Indian Road*, he sought to focus on an expression of the Gospel that India would understand. This he found, not in the Old Testament, nor the Christian church, and certainly not in Western civilization, but in Christ and him crucified. "A great people," he believed, "of amazing spiritual capacities is seeing, with remarkable insight that Christ is the center of Christianity" (1925:14). This view, he testified, came from his own spiritual renewal, so that he began to speak of Christ, not of Christianity, as the only way to deepen one's God-consciousness (44, 48). This is what Gandhi was reaching for, Jones believed, when he spoke of soul-force. Through their experience, Indians want to know if Christian experience is like that of the Bible. Jones returns at the close of his book to the theme, made prominent by the Hindu revival, of renewing India's traditions. How will this happen? Certainly not by holding on to old and decaying forms of spirituality. Rather, this spirituality must be brought to Christ.

> As that genius pours itself through Christian molds it will enrich the collective expression of Christianity. But in order to do that the Indian must remain Indian. He must stand in the stream of India's culture and life and let the force of that stream go through his soul so that the the expression of his Christianity will be essentially eastern (193).

These sentiments, closely tied to the nationalist movement, led Indian Christians to found the Christian Institute for Study of Religion and Society. Paul D. Devanandan (1901–1962), its founder, believed not in an adaptation to Hinduism but in the exploration of God's continuous activity in the world, which is renewing not only Indian traditions but the church as well (see England, ed., 1981:192). Another major figure of the Institute, M. M. Thomas, wrote *The Acknowledged Christ of the Indian Renaissance*, in which he defines theology as "the explication of the truth of the contemporary encounter between the Gospel and the situation" (1969:298). In another place Thomas surveys the common thread that unites much of contemporary Indian theology. Christ, he says, is the clue to a new understanding of humanity: "Jesus represents not merely the meeting, but the fusion into unity of God and man so that man may partake of it. It is thus that Christ becomes 'God permanently residing in creation' bringing to birth 'a new order in creation'" (in Anderson, ed., 1976:31). This new creation is not something that touches history from outside: it takes hold of the process of human history from within (ibid. 32).

One who has developed this reflection on humanity in the Indian context a step further is Samuel Rayan (1976; and see his article in England, ed., 1976:211–20). Men and women as created in the image of God in community (not individually), he believes, are the only images or symbols capable of pointing to the mystery of the divine with any depth. So only in waiting upon the mystery of this image can we come to discover the divine with an ever-deepening sense of the real. "Men and women in community are the only place of life-giving encounter and communion with God" [ibid., 213. Cf. Saral K. Chatterji's question: "Do the symbols and images of the Christians in India reflecting their faith relate in any way to the symbols of social relationships . . . of the People?" (1980:26)].

In another article Rayan ties this more closely to an understanding of history. The understanding of history in Hinduism has been largely cyclical: when one rides the cycles of karma, one becomes history. But the Bible is also cyclical: God's people move from captivity to freedom to captivity again (1976: 176, 185). In Scripture history is God's gift. Precisely because of his presence "history becomes a multi-dimensional reality of new depth and breadth" (186).

Now for the Christian, Rayan believes, the resurrection marks the beginning of the last days, a period in which Christ is present in a more radical way. "The eschaton [or the end of history] . . . is the inner dynamic of the world in process, and of human history moving toward its completion in Christ" (ibid., 188). So whenever a person responds to Christ, time moves forward, and that person becomes a part of the eschaton on earth. So, Rayan concludes, "the question about history is a question about the human" (189). What is truly historical is not mastery of the earth, but self-mastery. But here the Gospel challenges all our religious disciplines, for this healing cannot come from inside us: Romans 7 is the secret of history (191). God must put this love in us, and where it does not exist in relationships—e.g., in castes in India—God cannot be present. Interestingly he goes on to insist that this love must also have a public and political dimension (quoting Paulo Freire). But the human meaning of history must be a personal response to the presence of Christ.

These are only a few of the attempts of Indian theologians to rethink their faith in the Indian context. Evangelicals in general have been critical of these attempts. Sunand Sumithra and Bruce Nicholls, for example, concluded that Appasamy's "emphasis on the immanence of God without a corresponding emphasis on the transcendence of God in revelation leads to reductionism" (1983:178). Elsewhere Nicholls has criticized Appasamy for seeking a synthesis between the Bhakti tradition and Christianity that failed to bring that tradition into serious dialogue with biblical theology. He especially has in mind John's teaching on love. If Appasamy had done this, "we might have had a lasting and transformed use of Bhakti"—as Paul was able to use and transform the Greek idea of "mystery" (in Ro and Eshenaur, 1984:251).

M. M. Thomas likewise has been criticized for "ideologizing" the Gospel. "Starting with the analysis of the human situation [Thomas] uses Christ and the Church as a means in a programme of action" (Sumithra and Nicholls, 1984:180). In general, in the evangelical view, the religious orientation of the Hindu worldview and its openness to various mediations of the transcendent threatens Christianity's claim that Christ is the historically unique means of salvation.

At the same time Vinay Samuel and Chris Sugden wonder

whether Indian evangelicals have taken seriously enough the influence of their own thought forms on their theology. They also inquire whether evangelicals in general have considered how God might be present in other religions. "The goal," they insist, "is not to apply ready-made formulations of the Gospel, but to understand the focus, emphasis, and the very meaning of the biblical Gospel in that context" (1983:129).

The kind of careful interaction Samuel and Sugden propose is surely as urgent as it is unusual in India today. It is urgent because of the growing assimilation of Western secularism by Indian culture. As a result of this process, says Sunand Sumithra, formerly of Union Seminary, "the modern Indian lives in a cultural vacuum, or at least he lives in a multicultural situation" (in Ro and Eshenaur, 1984:226). But in spite of this, he notes, the common features of Hindu culture persist—including the caste system, worship of Hindu gods and goddesses with festivals and pilgrimages, and the general Hindu world picture. Nevertheless, a comprehensive attempt to take all these factors into account, along the lines proposed by Samuel and Sugden, still lies in the future. Sumithra concludes, "Wholistic contextualization taking into consideration the total preunderstanding of the receptor culture has not yet been attempted in India" (ibid., 225–26; cf. 238n11). We cannot propose what direction this discussion will take, but let us look more closely at the issue of Christ's relation to humanity, as an example of the thinking currently being done.

In general, Indian thinkers point out, Western thought patterns are fundamentally dualistic, therefore analysis is the primary mode of critical thought. Eastern patterns favor nondualistic modes, therefore thinking tends to be synthetic. S. J. Samartha in his book *The Hindu Response to the Unbound Christ* (1974 partially reprinted in Elwood, ed., 221–39) takes this "eastern pattern" as his starting point. He notes that "advaita" is the key—Sankara's system of Vedanta, which draws together God, world, and man in a single conception of unity. Now in the West doctrines about Christ have struggled with how to combine his two natures; Samartha wants to ask rather, "What is the Reality that one encounters in Jesus of

Nazareth as the living and risen Lord?" (in Elwood, ed., 1976:223). That is, starting with unity (and the basically positive response of Hinduism to Christ), we ask: How do we come to the realization and experience of the reconciliation that Christ brought not only to history but also to the cosmos itself? (ibid., 236). The emphasis is placed on God's intention, not to divide the race, but to unite it in Christ—not on Christ's uniqueness, but on his universality.

There are obvious limitations (and dangers!) to this way of thinking. But Samartha points out the limitations in our Western patterns as well: starting from distinctness and individualism, we have trouble understanding community, for example. Samartha, in fact, warns against a new bondage to Hindu culture. The Gospel, he believes, reveals limitations to thinking based on nonduality. Specifically, the Hindu world-view does not allow for the freedom and responsibility of the individual person (especially in the face of karma); it obscures the social and historical dimensions of human life; it disallows the appearance of the "new person" in history; and it underestimates the reality and intractable character of evil (ibid., 231–33). We will pick up this discussion below, but here it is already clear that commitment to Christ and his Word leads to a fundamental orientation toward the world that inevitably affects our worldview.

All this underlines the necessity of encouraging a genuine interaction between Scripture and the cultural context—an interaction in which Sripture is allowed to raise its own questions as well as respond to the questions of the context (cf. Sumithra and Nicholls, 176). But in this process it is important to allow Scripture to throw a new light, other than the light we have already found, on this unique context. Unfortunately, to this point not much serious biblical theology is apparent in the thinking we have surveyed.

Sri Lanka has a unique history and exhibits perhaps the purest form of Buddhism in Asia. Recent interaction with this tradition has thrown interesting light on the theology of the person. A Methodist theologian, Lynn A. de Silva, was among the first to probe very deeply in this tradition and to demonstrate a more serious interaction with Scripture. He came to believe that the three concepts of Buddha's analysis of existence offered important insights into humanity and the ground for a genuinely indigenous theology. Like Scripture, he noted, this analysis arose from an existential concern: *anicca* (impermanence), *anatta* (soullessness), and *dukkha* (suffering or existential anxiety) are indeed the three marks of human existence. Psalm 90 and Romans 8:18–25 suggest these are biblical concerns (theology, he claims, has now even abandoned the search for an "eternal soul"; cf. in Fabella, ed., 1980:99). Creation has to do essentially with dependence— and there is no escape from conditionedness. But how, in the Buddhist schema, can one reconcile *anicca* and *anatta* with the eternal working of karma? If there is no substantial personal entity, what is subject to this law?

What is lacking in the Buddhist analysis, de Silva insists, is provided by the biblical notion of *pneuma*, or spirit. Biblical theology agrees that the person as creature in itself is subject to decay (see the article in Ellwood, ed., 1976:111). But the person is created in God's image and thus can fulfill himself in relation to God. *Pneuma*, de Silva points out, is the biblical word that describes this relatedness. "Man is spirit only in relation to God who is Spirit" (ibid.). This relation is a fulfilling self-transcendence, not a negating one. The biblical idea of spirit, then, both profits from and fulfills anatta: the one stresses the relational dimension, the other its nonegocentric character (114).

Here is an important attempt to "correct" Buddhist insight by the truth of Scripture. The problem with Buddhist thinking on the person is its denial of any continuing or substantial reality to the self. While the Bible recognizes that all flesh is like grass, in the human spirit there is the capacity to transcend this conditionedness and respond to the voice of God. Sri Lankan evangelical Tissa Weerasingha believes de Silva does not stress sufficiently the "glaring disharmony" between Christianity and Buddhism that this difference in views suggests (in Ro and Eshenaur, 1984:300). De Silva, however, has taken an important step in making use of good biblical scholarship in his Buddhist context.

One who has added depth and richness to the relational view of humanity, still within a Buddhist framework, is Aloysius Pieris. Building on a Christological foundation, he believes that God can be sought only in total self-abnegation. Only in this way can one touch the depths of the human person, both one's own and that of others (1988:9). This is the essence of the Gospel: deny yourself and take up your cross. But this experience, in contrast to Buddhism, is a self-abnega-tion that grows into self-fulfillment (ibid., 10). With this starting point, Pieris develops a unique theology of poverty, one that gives it an important role in spirituality and adds a new perspective to the Latin American discussions. Spiritual-ity, Pieris argues, is the struggle to be poor, to deny oneself. Poverty was Jesus' characteristic posture toward both God and mammon (17). Both "poverties" involve a victory over selfishness—the one over the desire to be great, the other over that "subtle force operating within me, [that] inquisitive instinct" (16). Both are possible only because of Christ's own "spiritual poverty," which led to his death on the cross.

Pieris is anxious to make clear that this poverty will not leave the social realities unchanged—his book, after all, is entitled *A Liberation Theology for Asia*. Poverty in all its forms represents a spirituality of struggle. Voluntary poverty, however, is the seed of liberation; forced poverty is the fruit of sin (20). The poor by choice are the followers of Christ (Matt. 19:21); the poor by birth (or circumstance) are the proxies of Christ (14:31–46). What is renounced by one, then, belongs to the other. He summarizes: "The Kingdom of God can be viewed in terms of a universal practice of one [poverty] and consequent elimination of the other" (20). Speaking as a Jesuit, he notes that sacraments of history (examples of which are seen in the early chapters of Acts and later in the religious orders), in which everything is held in common, must recur in history many times before a dent can be made on human consciousness (he believes that in this we have much to learn from the Buddhist monks, 21).

While Pieris does not deny that social analysis and even political intervention may be necessary to Christian obedience, he adds an important dimension to the discussion of the spirituality of poverty, one that is nourished by the religious depth of his Buddhist setting.

CHINA AND THE QUESTION OF HISTORY

China has a long and noble history—it is perhaps the only country in the world to be politically and culturally united over more than three millennia. "It is only natural that China tended to become a self-contained, closed society whose history and culture tended to be strong and more influential" (Zhao Fusan, 1986:1). Although missionaries in the nineteenth century recognized this heritage, they did not see any need of appropriating it in their evangelism. Indeed, they tended to equate evangelization with conquest (Lam, 1983:28).

Early in this century the growing indigenous church was put on the defensive by the insatiable hunger of China for modernization and self-sufficiency. During these debates Christianity was identified sometimes with superstition, sometimes with imperialism. This opposition reached crisis proportions in the 1920s, challenging the church to respond. According to Wing-Hung Lam's dissertation on this period, the Christian response has been influential in all subsequent history. Strongly influenced by the revival tradition and an emphasis on the imitation of Christ and character formation, a Christocentric theology was developed (ibid., 30–45). This, Lam believes, was a strategic theological retreat designed to preserve the purity of the Gospel and come to terms with the practical side of Chinese nature, while avoiding the polemics both of the liberal-fundamentalist debate and of the Chinese antimodernists (ibid., 46, 154). This retreat has marked theological discussion to the present.

The idea was to take this theological kernel— Christlikeness—and contextualize it in the Chinese setting. But this process, beginning already in the 1920s, was carried on without any sustained dialogue with the religious and intellectual traditions of China. This was probably in part because of the mentality of retreat and also because these very traditions were under attack, first by the modernists and later by the Marxists. As a result Christian thought has been largely confessional and devotional rather than interpretive; therefore it has not reached the level of cultural identity (Elwood, 1975:10–11). As Wing-Tsit Chan puts this: "So long as Christianity fails to come in contact with Chinese intelligentsia, it will have failed to reach the nerve center of the Chinese people" (*Religious Trends in Modern China*, 2–3, quoted in ibid., 8–9). That Marxism itself has not reached to this level of identity may account for its current crisis in China.

It is increasingly obvious to students of modern China that this cultural identity is still primarily Confucian. Confucius was an administrator and teacher who lived from 551–479 B.C. His teachings, collected by his students in the *Analects* focus on benevolence or goodwill as the center of all virtue, even of life itself. He taught within a general Taoist framework —that is, belief in the Way (Tao), or cosmic order, that permeates and animates all reality. For Confucius this Way was primarily to be expressed in terms of family and filial piety or reverence, the most exalted virtue and center of all good works (Chao, 1987:22). Indeed, the welfare of the state and the people depended on the right ordering of the family. Confucius seemed to have been unsure about God's existence, recognizing him more as an abstract concept of nature than as a person (ibid., 25). But above all, Confucius was a humanist who sought to develop true humanity through study and the martial arts, which were felt to achieve a unity between earth and heaven.

These ideas have been influential throughout Chinese history and have been reformulated by the neo-Confucians of the eleventh to the thirteenth centuries A.D. as well as by contemporary scholars (such as Wing-Tsit Chan). For these, salvation and fullness of life are to be found in the regular round of daily life. As in the familiar Chinese brushwork paintings, people are found playing their humble role amidst fields, streams, and mountain peaks. This poem by neo-Confucian Ch'eng Hao captures the Confucian gospel of faithfulness to one's daily activities:

> These later years have brought me
>   Quietude of life.
> My eastern window reddens,
>   I awake.
>
> The world a vision is,
>   Stillness self-revealed.
> This season, fair to view,
>   To man akin.
>
> The word doth pierce the corporeal world,
>   Itself without a form.
> Thought enters wind and cloud,
>   Changing with them.
>
> The pride and pomp of life
>   Brings me no vicious joy.
> Thus I am a man, no more,
>   And thus a hero amongst men.
>
>   (quoted in Fung, 1962:201)

Perhaps the most influential theologian working within this framework is the Taiwanese theologian Choan-Seng Song. A member of the Reformed Church in Taiwan, Song was educated there and at New College in Edinburgh. After a term as associate director of the Faith and Order Commission of the World Council of Churches, he has come to Berkeley, California, as a professor in the Pacific School of Religion. This revival of traditional Chinese culture, he believes, has opened new possibilities for Christian theology. Within this framework he proposes a theology of the Incarnation, which he defines as the eternal presence of a powerfully creative force, truth meeting truths deep in creation and history (in Anderson, ed., 1976:155). He wants to show "how the creative power of God's saving love is at work even in the darkest corner of the world" (ibid., 157–58).

He elaborates this thesis in a series of influential books. In the first (1975) he seeks to "reconstruct" the Christian mission in the relational context of Asia. Consistent with his Reformed perspective, he wants to connect redemption to creation and thus release Christ "from the captivity of the so-called [holy history] and set him in the process of history as the continuation of the work of creation" (1975:35). Starting with the depths of Asia's experience, which he, following Buddha, qualifies as suffering, he wants to show that "the intrinsic meaning of each historical entity has its origin in God the creator" (ibid., 33). The church in Asia must be willing to lose itself in these depths so that justice and love may be made visible. Thus participating in Christ, the church will overcome the particularities of mission. This leads Song to a unique interpretation of Christ's incarnation: in Christ, God's larger purposes of transforming chaos and dispelling darkness have been set loose in every cultural setting. Only this perspective, he believes, will allow us to overcome the particularistic interpretation of mission. The dynamics of history, as of mission, after all, are the dynamics of creation.

One can see clearly the influence of Song's Confucian framework. He wants to locate salvation not primarily in political or cultural dynamics, but in the human depths. In 1984 in *Tell Us Our Names* he elaborated this humanistic tradition in terms of incarnation. The truth of Christianity has its fulcrum in "the word becoming flesh, God becoming a human person . . . the life and history of God becoming the life and history of human beings" (1984:9). We must be agents of this insight, telling people their names, helping them see that "in life, each of us encounters the shame, pain and death of the cross, but at the same time we experience the glory, joy and life of resurrection" (ibid., 19). Later (1986) Song seeks to elicit this life of God from the fabric of Asian life. Deep in the heart of Asia there are codes—Hong Kong 1997, Hiroshima, Vietnam; who will decode these things? The Christian is to bring a vision of God's reign to all this, a space in the margin of life (1986:206). But this vision will not come necessarily via Christian images (he is anxious to slough off the particularity of revelation; ibid., 36). It may even come through the Asian mask dances, in which people transcend themselves and their conditions and come to grips with their problems, gaining strength to solve them (219).

Song is eloquent in recording the Asians' passion and longing that must in the end animate a living faith and equally eloquent in setting these beside the stark images of Scripture. But he is so anxious to avoid the conflict resulting from the institutional (and cultural) baggage the missionaries brought to Asia, that he too, like China in the 1920s, stages a theological retreat. Christ is the key to a peoples' suffering; Christ is present in the depths of these cries. Here we have an interesting variation on Segundo's disposal of sacred history. That particular history stopped with Christ, and he became one with all human projects working for justice. Song is less interested in these political struggles than in the personal and human cries for deliverance he hears in Asia. But is there no way to identify particular places where God is working? Just how is Christ present in all suffering? Like flouride in water? If Christ is present in the same way wherever people are hurting, has the meaning of this presence been reduced?

In the light of modern Chinese history it is hard to miss the irony of this retreat. In the 1920s Christianity was suspect because it was thought to be in conflict with the scientific worldview; it was considered a superstition like Confucianism (also out of fashion). But fashion changes. Now a reaction to both Marxist and capitalist materialism is sweeping Asia. People want a return to their heritage; they hunger for a deep humanization. But few (especially in China) want this at the cost of "modernization": they want to hold on to their Hong Kongs as creative financial and business centers. How can these desires be held together? The deep and authentic humanization they long for certainly cannot be achieved by giving up the responsibility for working in history. This human ability, it could be argued, rests on the view of history that centers in Christ's life and death. Setting goals and working toward them is of the essence of modern experimental science and technology. Do these in some way reflect God's own project, which worked with particular people and in particular places? Yet it seems that it is just such particularity that Song is anxious to jettison. Does he realize what is at stake?

Mircea Eliade has pointed out that most non-Western historiography relies on exemplary patterns. This is because there is no sense of history as unrepeatable events. "Every *event* (every occurrence with any meaning), simply by being *effected in time*, represents a break in profane time and an irruption of the Great Time" (1958:396, his emphases). Thus history cannot be anything more than exemplary patterns, of which Christ's death, in Song's conception, is only the most significant. It becomes a kind of mythical event that takes place outside of history and thus becomes "exemplar history for the human society in which [it] has been preserved, and for the world that society lives in" (ibid., 430). The meaning of these events lies in their very repeatability. But according to Scripture, the meaning of Christ's death lies in its character as a single sacrifice (see Hebrews 10); its very essence lies in its uniqueness. The particularity of this story, moreover, lies at the basis of the whole Western conception of history (rather than Western thought patterns having produced this understanding). As Geoffrey Parrinder notes, "True appreciation of history begins with the man Christ Jesus, the word made flesh" (1982:278). In fact, one might argue that Song has not altered the fundamental monism of the Hindu (or Taoist) worldview at all; he has merely replaced the Hindu mythology with a Christian one—it is Christ rather than Vishnu who works out the order of reality. His project of de-Westernization of Christianity (cf. 1975:67) has not left the Gospel any leverage to transform his own setting.

There are those who argue that these Eastern patterns of thought are inviolable and Christianity must adapt to them completely. Jung Young Lee has argued that in Asia we must get out of the habit of thinking in terms of either/or; we must be able to think of both/and. Change, he believes, may be the key to the universe, and ambiguity and differences merely the reflection of aspects of reality. In traditional Chinese thought, *yin* and *yang* are believed to be complementary modes of being—the shadow (female), passive on the one hand; and the bright (male), active on the other (in Elwood, ed. 1976:59–65 see also Lee, 1974, where he seeks to apply this to his view of God). This type of thinking, Lee demands (with an un-Asian dogmatism), "must be adopted by theology" (ibid., 65).

Clearly there is a tolerance for ambiguity that Westerners can learn from—as a student of mine once commented, "Why do you Westerners always have to understand and control the world? Why can't you contemplate it and sing with it?" But the ability to locate truth in a particular history may be more than a Western habit of thought; it may relate to the way God has made himself known. The Eastern and Western ways, in this case, may not be cultural habits alone, but may relate to basic, and fundamentally opposed, ways of conceiving God's relation to the world. This question calls for further discussion below.

JAPAN AND THE NATURE OF SPIRITUALITY

In one sense, as Pierce Beaver notes, none of the generalities of Asia apply to Japan. It is ancient, medieval, and modern; it is Eastern and Western. And all these characteristics exist in dynamic interrelationship (see Drummond, 1971:9).

But, like other Asian countries with noble traditions, Japan won immediate respect from early missionaries. Francis Xavier wrote in 1549: "They are the best race yet discovered, and I think that among non-Christians their match will not easily be found. Admirable in their social relationships, they have an astonishing sense of honor and esteem it above all other things. . . . the Japanese are full of courtesy in their dealings with one another [and] take pleasure in hearing of the things of God" (quoted in ibid., 15).

The Catholic mission that Xavier began was not successful in terms of numbers, but it has figured prominently in Japanese history. Because of rigorous attempts to suppress Christianity, and the extreme torture administered to believers who were found out, Christians in the sixteenth and seventeenth centuries were forced underground. When found out, they were made to step on an image of Christ (the *fumie*); if they refused, they were persecuted and killed. This period of terror and persecution has captured the imagination of Japanese and is remembered in their art and, as we will see, even in their contemporary literature.

Protestants did not arrive until the mid-nineteenth century, but the first Protestant missionaries were of a high standard and became very influential. Guido Verbeck, for example, began a school that was to educate a surprising number of the makers of modern Japan (Drummond, 147, 153). For these reasons the Japanese church, though consistently small, has had able and well-trained leadership from the beginning and so has avoided some of the problems of missionary paternalism and Western influence.

The Japanese religious interest, which Xavier commented on, derived from ancient Shintoism, which has interesting similarities to both Hinduism and Taoism. It has a similar meta-cosmic orientation that ascribes sacred power to natural objects or people insofar as they participate in the force (or *kami*) that is from above (cf. ibid., 22). This was altered by the introduction of Buddhism in the sixth century A.D. Buddhism in Asia has had the unique capacity to adapt itself to the many different settings to which it has come, and in every case it is perceived to be indigenous. In Japan this has taken the form of several "schools," the best known of which is Zen Buddhism, popularized in the West by Japanese scholar D. T. Suzuki.

A characteristic feature of Zen Buddhism, important for understanding Japanese theology, is that insight (or illumination) is not achieved by some course of study or even by some particular spiritual discipline or religious path. Salvation comes through sudden inspiration. This can come about through an ordinary experience or an encounter with an everyday object, an event that "triggers" illumination into the depths of reality. The Zen masters, in fact, seemed quite purposefully to turn attention away from the great and lofty toward the humble and mundane. The famous Haiku poems (of exactly seventeen syllables) were meant to stimulate this experience of what is at the heart of nature:

> Breaking the silence
> Of an ancient pond,
> A frog jumped into water—
> A deep resonance.
>
> (Basho in Song 1986:57)

This deep meditative stance toward the world and this history of profound suffering have given Japanese Christian reflection a unique character. Kazoh Kitamori, one of the best known Japanese theologians since the war, embodies both of these characteristics. He has an extremely wide knowledge of Japanese traditions. For many years he suffered from tuberculosis, and from this experience and the anguish of national defeat in World War II he wrote *A Theology of the Pain of God* (1946, ET 1965).

Taking his departure from Jeremiah 31:20 ("My heart yearns [lit. is in pain] for [Ephraim]; I have great compassion for him"), Kitamori reflects on the nature of God. "Ever since this strange word ['yearns'] struck me," he confesses, "I have meditated on it night and day" (1965:151). The results of his meditation form the substance of this book.

The pain of God for Kitamori is a concept of relation, not a part of God's essence (ibid., 16). It is reflective of his love. For contrary to what liberal theology has taught since Schleiermacher, God cannot embrace us immediately. He must love us mediately, that is through his pain (24). "The pain of God reflects his will to love the object of his wrath" (21). But Kitamori insists that this love must conquer his wrath in the midst of history. The suffering of Jesus, then, is implied in God's pain (34); it is an act within God. So the essence of God can be comprehended only by "the word of the cross" (47).

Human pain, then, takes on a new importance. It represents the reality of our estrangement from God (60–61), but it can be the means of learning about God's pain and even become a vehicle of service to him: "There are two ways to render service to the pain of God. The first is to let our *loved ones* suffer and die. The second is for *us* to suffer and die. The first witnesses to the 'pain of *God*' the second to the '*pain* of God' " (81).

Kitamori did not mean to make this a new framework for theology and soon moved beyond it (cf. Adams 1987:54–56). But for postwar Japan it was an important statement. It picked up the Buddhist theme of healing through suffering and mined the deep interpersonal empathy possible in Japanese culture— in Japanese drama the concept of "Tsurasa," a deep personal agony suffered for others, is central. For the Japanese the fundamental human tragedy is one of human relationship (135). As Japanese playgoers weep shamelessly at the cries of agony of the players, so they have the capacity to feel something of the deep pain of God, who suffered for a fallen world.

Theologically, Kitamori understood that the Gospel transcends even this Japanese sympathy, for God's pain involves loving the unlovable as well as the lovely—something strange to Japanese culture (138). But Kitamori believed this sensitivity could provide a vehicle for experiencing God's loving embrace of a fallen world. He seems to understand that God's character transcends this ability to suffer—it is a concept of relation, not of essence (though the resurrection is not given any prominence in this discussion). But he believes that the knowledge of God in a fallen world and a relationship with him, at least for Asians, are frequently mediated by suffering.

In Japan it has occasionally been the novelists who capture the dramatic value of Christ's suffering for the Japanese (since the war a number of the leading novelists have been Christian). A good example is Shusako Endo (b. 1923), a Catholic influenced by the writers of the French Catholic revival in literature (François Mauriac and George Bernanos, among others). His own experience of belonging to the religion of the enemy during the war led him to look on himself as a coward and an outsider and thus to feel deeply the central Japanese tragedy of painful relationships.

In *Silence* (1969) he portrays the tragedy of betrayal in the light of the existence of a loving God. Set amidst the suffering of seventeenth-century Christians, Rodriguez, a Portuguese priest, comes secretly to Japan to discover why an earlier missionary, Father Ferreira, had apostasized. He comes to realize the depths of suffering—and betrayal—that Christians were experiencing. Once, after he has discovered the insidious means of the torturers, he stands gazing out on the sea that had—with unchanging expression—swallowed up two of the Christians. "And like the sea, God was silent. His silence continued" (1969:117). He discovers Ferreira just at the point where he can no longer stand the water torture inflicted on the Christians. As the apostate priest watches, he is told to trample on the image of Christ in order to save the lives of Christians. "Your brethren in the Church will judge you as they have judged me," says Ferreira. "But there is something more important than the Church, more important than missionary work: what you are about to do" (ibid., 270). As he is about to step on the *fumie*, the face of Christ speaks: "Trample! Trample! I more than anyone know of the pain in your foot. Trample! It was to be trampled on by men that I was born into this world. It was to share men's pain that I carried my cross" (271).

On the surface this is the story of deep failure, and Western readers are typically troubled by this aspect. But there is a deeper question here: How is success to be measured? By fortitude alone? For us in the West, it is so; ours is a spirituality of strength and conquest. But spirituality in Asia may be one of *tsurasa*—a deep pain for the sake of others. Could experiences like this trigger a deeper awareness of God?

Masao Takenaka is a Japanese theologian who believes that such experiences are the secret not only of our relation to God but also of a new theological method. Making much use of art and drama, Takenaka calls the argumentative method of theology in the West the "Ya-ya" method. "Whenever two or three Western theologians are gathered together, there is argumentation about God," he jokes (1986:8). As an alternative to this, he proposes the "Ah-hah!" method. In the Bible, he argues, people did not come to know God by discussion or argument, but by experiencing him. "We must awaken in ourselves the appreciation of the living reality who is God. In the Bible we have many surprising acknowledgements.. . .'Ah-hah! In this way, God is working in our world, in a way I did not know' " (ibid., 9).

This means developing deep sensitivity toward the "at-mosphere" of the place where we live, as the basis for knowing God (16). Only in this way will we begin to perceive the presence of God, as this Haiku poem expresses this awareness of place:

> The budding plum
> Holds my own joy
> At the melting of ice
> And the long winter's end.
> (Ikuko Uchida in ibid, 27).

All of Japanese art, Takenaka reminds us, grows from a basic characteristic of Japanese life called *wabi*. This is beauty expressed without pretension, in a meek spirit and with harmony. It is seen above all in the art of flower arranging or in the Japanese tea ceremony. Takenaka believes that Christ can best be understood by Japanese in these terms. He often kept silence, he wept at death, he was troubled, and he found his friends in table fellowship—this is the attitude of mind, Paul says in Philippians 2, that we are to have (78–82).

So Kitamori and Takenaka portray the two sides of the sense of *hibiki*, the depth of nature and humanity. The secret of the deep pain we feel can only be found with Jesus on the cross. But the secret of the deep joy we know must be found in him as well, for "in him was life, and that life was the light of men" (John 1:4).

One who tries to hold these dimensions together is Kosuke Koyama, a student of Kitamori. He later became a missionary to Thailand and is now professor of ecumenics at Union Seminary in New York. His 1974 book *Waterbuffalo Theology*, written in the Buddhist context of Thailand, had something of the same impact of Gutiérrez' book of the previous year. It opened a whole new universe of theological discussion that focused many of the themes we have considered.

Koyama's primary emphasis is on the importance of the concrete context for thinking about God. "On my way to the country church, I never fail to see a herd of waterbuffaloes grazing in the muddy paddy field. The watebuffaloes tell me that I must preach to these farmers [with] objects that are immediately tangible. . .'sticky rice'. . .'rainy season,' 'leaking house'" (1974:vii). This concrete, and sometimes painful, project of living must be allowed to raise questions that provide an entrance for the Gospel. This project too is the primary truth of history. Like the other Asian theologians we have been considering, he sees history in terms of nature, not the reverse. It is surprising, he notes, how "a bank account and an abundant diet somehow . . . insulate man from coming to feel the primary truth of history" (ibid., 23).

This suggests a different theological method from that practiced in the West. Starting from a full stomach (which, as Latin American theologians have reminded us, is part of our presuppositions), we assume order. Starting from a situation that hurts or bothers, as in Asia, perhaps we will assume disorder. Why, asks Koyama, do we always ask cool living-room questions, and not hot kitchen questions? What if we moved theology from the living room to the kitchen? (ibid., 79–83. Note that, in general, creation accounts in the Old Testament, reflecting a general ancient Near Eastern pattern, move from chaos to order, not the reverse).

Then should we perhaps season our inquiry with a dose of ambiguity and patience? No, Koyama tells us slyly, there are no instant solutions. This theme he picks up in *No Handle on the Cross* (1976). God does not work in straight lines; he does not provide handles by which to carry his cross. The finality of Jesus is that he was spat on (1976:93). When we think that the most efficient civilizations today spend billions of dollars on arms annually, suddenly, Koyama says, the cross appears downright efficient.

Unlike many Asian theologians, Koyama believes that the Gospel and Buddhism provide two opposing solutions to our historical situation. The Buddha says that we should not allow "like and dislike to arise." But, says Koyama, as long as even the illusion of desire exists, we are not free from passion (ibid., 140–41). God's solution is not *apatheia*, but *patheia*, attachment to history, which Scripture calls the covenant. In Christ "chaos and darkness are overcome. A new creation takes place. . . . In Christ, man began to see the glory of God not as the man who aspires to reach beyond history, but as a man who lives in history" (152).

But this should not lead us to a smug sense of superiority that glories in the "rottenness of Buddhism." Koyama lashes out against all "self-admiration theology." This has no place in the Gospel: "Boast of the crucified Lord! How can one boast of the crucified Lord with the crusading mind and crusading solution?" (ibid., 41). Note how this Christian attitude is grounded in his basic theological commitment to the Gospel. Christ achieved victory through accepting defeat; how can this lead to a crusading mind? (8).

What is the victory that Christ achieved? At the death of Christ the whole creation was brought into "crisis in order to exist in the new quality of time henceforth. The risen Lord means, then, the coming of the new time, the new order, the new covenant, the new humanity" (ibid., 112). We who have experienced this unusual disruption of time, can live, then, not only with a crucified mind, but also with a risen mind.

It seems that Koyama does more than many other Asian theologians to preserve an actual historical intervention in Christ's work that changed the moral and spiritual order of things. But some are still troubled by his insistence that the finality of Christ cannot be proved even by a hundred quotations from the Bible. Finality takes place only within ourselves when we respond to the basic questions: Do you hear? Do you see? "It takes place when ordinary hearing and seeing are penetrated by an extraordinary hearing and seeing" (1976:1). This is consistent with the Japanese feeling that insight must be provoked rather than argued. At the same time it recalls John Calvin's assertion that it is not ultimately the evidences (what he called the *indicia*), but the internal witness of the Holy Spirit that gives the certainty we yearn for. It also recalls the method Jesus himself used when he concluded his stories: "The ones who have ears, let them hear."

We are tempted to say that Koyama makes progress in communicating the Gospel, but not in formulating (or testing) it. Although there is some truth in this, Koyama needs to be understood in his context. For Asians, thinking in images is not a strategy of communication (like sermon illustrations to drive home a point); it is a special mode of thought that is at home with proverbs and parables, which make up in evocative power what they lose in precision.

We are uncomfortable with this because it seems to allow unnecessary uncertainty and imprecision. Is our refusal to allow ambiguity partly cultural? Jesus at times did not seem overly concerned with it: "Whoever is not against you is for you," he said to his worried disciples (Luke 9:49). Is it that precise formulations are not possible in a fallen order or that our precision is more of an approximation than we have thought?

But we may not leave matters there. Surely something is to be gained by the push to precision. Koyama's questions are good ones, but I often have some to ask in return. I often wonder how the images, and his chapters, relate to one another. The covenant is a radical ("hot") attachment to history, fine; but does this not have some implications for the finality of Christ? To be "spat upon" is not the only, or even the primary, biblical image of Christ's supremacy. There is also his kingly lordship that calls people to bow before him and will transform history. S. J. Samartha, in the book I have referred to, notes that a fundamental problem in Asian thinking is that the development of the Brahman is a harmonious and determined process. And the law of karma is inviolable. The temptation is to see Christ in terms of a similar inevitability. But Christ, Samartha points out, is an active personal agent in redemption and the new creation. Under his lordship it is not the "push of process" but the "pull of purpose" that is determinative (in Elwood, ed., 1976:230). This sense of Christ as the living Lord of history must illuminate

Christ as the spat-upon one, and, while it should not make us arrogant, it may give us confidence.

This Lord has intrigued the Japanese for centuries. But, at least since the war, the business of modern life has squeezed him into the periphery of things. The Japanese have fallen victim to the same technological captivity that afflicts us in the West—and which Koyama probes and teases. For these and other reasons, a church type of Christianity is in serious crisis in Japan (see Nabetani, 1983:75). Only 1 percent (or 1.2 million) belong to regular churches, though an equal number who attend no regular church also claim to be Christians. Especially around the prestigious Tokyo University many meet to pray and read the Bible while rejecting the church (ibid., 76–78). This is troublesome to many missionaries and Japanese Christians. But it represents yet another dimension of the challenge of Asian spirituality. How is it possible to channel and hold the seething depths of feeling? Perhaps this is what Endo's priest Ferreira meant when he said: "There is something more important than the church. . . ."

PHILIPPINES AND SOUTHEAST ASIA

Of the vast area of Southeast Asia referred to as lowland wet-rice cultures, we focus on the Philippines. These countries—Indonesia, Malaysia, and Thailand—differ widely from each other, but there are similarities as well. In all these the cosmic (animist) religions exist in uneasy relation to the major religious traditions and all the people of these countries struggle to modernize their economies without losing the spirituality of traditional values.

The values of the Filipino culture are personalistic and holistic. In one sense the overt religious (or meta-cosmic) orientation in the rest of Asia is missing here; in another sense the same monistic worldview is expressed in social relations. In any case Filipino personal values clearly express an Asian spirituality and are best explained in the larger Asian context we have been considering. Anthropologist Frank Lynch argued that Filipino values are organized around the desire for social harmony (what he called smooth interpersonal relations; 1964:5–10). Jaime Bulato (in Lynch, ed., 1964:50ff.) described this as the desire for emotional closeness and security in the family. These basic values are reflected in social relations through equivalence (each individual represents the whole group), solidarity (members unite against outsiders), and reciprocity (every service demands a return service) (ibid., 19–21).

Later studies have placed more emphasis on shame (*hiya*), which is based on self-esteem and sensitivity to personal affront, and on fate (*palod*) as the two poles around which behavior is organized (see the discussion in Tano, 1983). As we will see, this framework allows theological reflection to deal with the issues of personal responsibility in relation to the coming of modernization. It raises questions along the following lines: Is this "new" (i.e., modern) world in some way meant to reflect the new creation that Christ initiated? Does it destroy the old attitude of *bahala na* (that is the way things are so there is nothing we can do)?

During the Asian Theological Conference in Sri Lanka in 1979, it was formally recognized that there are really two Asias. One is represented by those countries (India, China, Japan) that are immersed in the major religious traditions. The second is represented by countries, such as the Philippines, that are dominated by the neocolonialism of technology and modernization (Fabella, ed., 1980:11). The Filipino theologians in particular reacted against Pieris' notion that theology in Asia must revolve around the poles of religiosity and poverty. In contrast to an emphasis on "religiosity," they believed the "main and principal characteristic of a truly Asian theology is its third worldness" (ibid., 194).

What constitutes "third worldness"? One answer is given by Filipino Methodist Emerito Nacpil, who has articulated a "critical Asian principle." This definition grew out of meetings in the early 1970s concerned with making theological education relevant to Asia (see Elwood, ed., 1976:3–6). The discussions attempted to define characteristics of Asian nations generally: their colonial experience, their living religions, and their vast social problems. All of these together were to be taken as a new frame of reference. They provided, Nacpil believed, a situational principle to indicate responsibilities; a hermeneutical principle—"we must understand the Gospel and the Christian tradition with these realities" (5); and a missiological and an educational principle that will give shape to their programs.

In other places Nacpil elaborates what he calls this critical Asian principle. For Filipinos, he believes, the Gospel provides liberation and a horizon of hope: "It is clear that nature must be swept clean of its spirits and demons and the world disenchanted and secularized" (Anderson, ed., 1976:126). In the 1977 All Asia Conference on Theological Education in Manila, Nacpil asked: What is the New Person of the modernization taking place today? Goals that originally came from the West are being adapted in Asia. This requires a new sense of rationality, efficiency, and cooperativeness. It requires people who can live with change and react as individuals. Christianity provides a fresh perspective on what it means to be a human: one who is living toward the future as a trustee of creation. This dynamic comes from the resurrection, which provides for "a fundamental alteration in the character and movement of history" (Nacpil and Elwood, eds., 1978:310; cf. 291–311). Notice how these issues confront the fundamental Filipino values listed above. Not only have people been delivered from the rule of fate, they have also been transformed into the agents of history.

It is interesting that these emphases were not appreciated in the later (1979) conference in Sri Lanka. Virginia Fabella commented that Nacpil's critical Asian principle "did not solve the problem of 'authenticity' and 'relevance'" (Fabella, ed., 1980:5). Indeed she concluded that the 1977 conference in Manila "failed to work on Asian realities, and in general . . . remained abstract and academic and dependent on Western sources" (ibid.). One wonders to what extent these negative judgments reflect the uniqueness of the Philippines within its Asian setting.

Perhaps this uniqueness provides an opportunity for innovation. In many ways the Philippines represents a special workshop for Third World theology: It is largely Christian, it has shared with Latin America the hunger for political liberation, and its presence in Asia has given it a unique sensitivity for spiritual and human values. But, unlike any other area of the Third World, it displays a positive attitude toward the processes of modernization. This is even seen as making possible an "Asian social transformation" (Arevalo in Nacpil and Elwood, eds., 1978:194).

This mix of issues has been dealt with fully by the Catholic theologians at the Loyola House of Studies in Manila. Father C. G. Arevalo, for example, has written an important article, "Theology of Development," using the Incarnation as the primary model (Elwood, ed., 1976:398–424). The influence of liberation theology on these thinkers is evident, but as we saw in our discussion of Latin American theology, they have taken the lead in critical discussions about the social analysis used by liberation theology (see Elwood, 1987, and Lambino et al., 1977). Antonio Lambino notes that theology must begin by formulating the imperatives (as opposed to simply the principles) of one's own situation that correspond to the struggle of the people to find life (in Nacpil and Elwood, eds., 1978:196). And Carlos Abesamis has done important work toward developing a catechism that relates these struggles to the Gospel and Christ's work (see Abesamis, 1988).

Let us look more closely at the thinking of C. G. Arevalo, who has become a major theological figure in Catholic Asia. First, Father Arevalo defines the task of theology as Christian reflection in the service of the Christian community itself (Lambino et al., 1977:113). This is an activity that flows from the community of faith into life and practice. Thus, though it is situated within the Christian community, it is oriented toward the world.

Second, Arevalo takes full account of the spiritual dimension of Asian and especially of Filipino values. "May I suggest that we look upon our people, in their poverty, in their hunger, in their need for literacy, for education, for opportunity, for liberty, as the little child . . . in whom Mozart lies sleeping . . . a hundred geniuses whose creativity is meant to enrich the world" (Elwood, ed., 1976:406–7).

Then we must engage in a genuine interaction with other frameworks and other settings (Why not use, he asks, even Western frameworks as working hypotheses when it is suitable?). In this way, "by asking very concrete questions raised from within real situations Asian Christians and Christian communities face, little by little . . . [we may] allow our own larger themes (and our own major framework) to emerge" (in Nacpil and Elwood, 1978:197). But this must be a functional theology that has an evangelical character. "What is called for is something that *internalizes* the lot of people caught in situations of poverty and hopelessness" (ibid., 199, their emphasis). A token experience will not do (the conference in Sri Lanka began with a much-discussed weekend experience among various poor communities!). Although Arevalo has clearly learned from liberation theology, the response to situations of hopelessness must not be one of moral outrage alone. It must consist of "the really difficult effort of hard-nosed multi-disciplinary research, analysis, step by step planning, as well as the exercise of 'utopian imagination'" (ibid.).

Central to all this is the practice of evangelical love and a formation of a spirituality of ministry that is integrated with worship, prayer, and obedience to God's will (201–3).

In his conclusion, though he does not make explicit reference to his Filipino setting, he faces the two fundamental themes exhibited in this culture: shame and fate. What we need above all, he argues, is a theology of human responsibility and of history that grows out of a Christology of servant-hood and sonship that responds to the actual situation of Asia in its transition from traditional to modernized societies (204–9).

Theological discussions like this are often dismissed because they do not appear on the scene in an innovative (and perhaps angry or threatening) way. But I wonder whether this (typically Filipino!) humility and willingness to learn from other parts of the Third World (even from the West!), when coupled with a deep concern about their Asian setting and a desire to serve God's people as they struggle to make a transition to the modern world, may not be an important model of theological method.

Karl Barth said somewhere that Christians should learn to say (and do) things in a kind and loving way that matches the content of their message. Asian theologians seem to have learned that lesson and propose methods of communication embodying the spirituality that should characterize all our life. Evangelical theologian David Lim of Manila, for example, proposes a "cross-ethic" that "emphasizes that good morals serve the concerns of the needy. It seeks to motivate and mobilize 'true spirituality' so that through calvary-love actions more human conditions of life may prevail" (1986:2).

CONCLUSION: WHAT HAVE WE LEARNED FROM ASIA?

Evangelicals have found interaction with Asian situations more difficult than with any other. The difficulties faced were laid out in the Seoul Declaration:

> We must proclaim the finality of Jesus Christ in the context of the universalistic and syncretistic tendencies expressed in some Asian theologies. The distinctive Asian qualities of spirituality, meditation and devotion, self-sacrifice and servanthood are to be tested and utilized in developing our theology (1983:11).

This statement itself expresses ambivalence: a wariness of the worldviews but an appreciation of the disciplines and sensitivities that have developed. But the deeper question still has to be faced: Can the disciplines and the underlying worldviews be separated in Asia? Aloysius Pieris insists they cannot—change must be 'religiously motivated.' This is to say that people will not respond "unless their lives are touched and their depths stirred by its prospects *along the cultural patterns of their own 'religious' histories,* for it seeks to explore and develop extensively the common ground between Christianity and Asian faiths." (1988:100, his emphasis). Vinay Samuel and Chris Sugden agree: "In the context of religious pluralism, no social change can take place without a religious reality that promotes this change" (1983:129). In Latin America and Africa studies of sociology and linguistics have been essential for mission advance, in Asia the philosophical and religious issues are inescapable.

In Asia, then, discussions of theology (even of missiology) will inevitably lead to the question of interreligious dialogue (see the discussion in Stott, 1975—chapter 3 on dialogue). Moreover, in Asia this dialogue will focus on the nature and role of transcendent (what Pieris has called the "meta-cosmic") faiths. For Asian Christians this will raise particular questions: What obstacles to the Gospel do Eastern worldviews present? How may these frameworks be enlisted in the work of constructive theology? And how does commitment to Christ alter these worldviews?

Clearly this dialogue goes beyond the level of evangelistic strategy, for it seeks to explore, not the uniqueness but the common ground. Unfortunately the record of serious evangelical interaction with the major religions has not been good. Reasons for this range from the long-standing isolation of many Western Christians to the superficial preparation of missionaries sent to these Asian countries. But Samuel and Sugden suggest a deeper reason:

> Evangelicals have tended to be a-historical, because they think in terms of belief systems. They have not really taken the historicity of Christian revelation seriously. So when they think of other religions they also tend not to take their historicity seriously. But if the event of Christ was decisive for all history, then the world of religions as part of history is affected by it. Our agenda is to discern how. (1983:139)

Obviously a thorough discussion of these issues lies beyond the scope of this book, but we may note briefly two directions such a dialogue might take—those that Pieris, on the one hand, and Samuel and Sugden on the other, might suggest. The route preferred by many Asian theologians is best articulated by Aloysius Pieris. He calls the process of bringing Christianity to Asia "inreligionization."

Pieris takes the position that religious change typically takes place from the cosmic religions to meta-cosmic faiths. The common characteristic of the latter faith is that it is "soteriological," or liberative of the person (1988:54, 107). If, then, there is an encounter between two meta-cosmic faiths, say between Christianity and Hinduism, there must be an "internal collaboration" that starts with the conception of salvation (not with God-talk!). For these religions already contain the revolutionary instinct to "humanize what has merely been hominized" (the language is that of Teilhard de Chardin, though he is not cited; ibid., 107). Christians in their involvement with such faiths must "assimilate" them as they participate in their ethos. This process Pieris likens to Jesus' allowing himself to be baptized in the Jordan, thus assimilating himself to John's preaching (55).

In Asia, then, Christianity must find its indigenous identity from within these soteriological faiths. Pieris argues that this is because conversion, properly speaking, takes place from cosmic to meta-cosmic faiths; it does not take place, without coercion, from one meta-cosmic faith to another. It is not clear whether for Pieris the liberation that Hindus seek is available only in Christ, or whether the liberation is actually the same experience that Christians know. It is possible that Pieris would dismiss such questions as "word games": "The word game about nature and person or the mathematics of one and three have only generated centuries of verbosity. It is wordlessness that gives every word its meaning" (ibid., 85). Pieris believes we must immerse ourselves in this Asian consciousness so that afterwards we can speak of Christ (God-talk, which is always secondary to the salvific experience) *in these terms.*

Evangelicals, following the suggestions of Samuel and Sugden, it seems to me, would take quite a different tack in their dialogue. We might start, for example, with the common perception (of Christians and Hindus) of the ultimacy of spiritual reality and the secondary and dependent nature of the physical world. We might even agree to start with the centrality of experience with "God," since this is important both to the Christian and to the Asian way of thinking. But even at this level, it might appear that the shape or contour of this central experience might be radically different and that this difference might in fact affect our orientation toward reality, even our thought patterns and ethical values. This fact might be recognized without any attempt, at this stage, to determine which experience is truer.

Let me attempt to elaborate this second mode of dialogue. Take, by way of illustration, the common understanding that Christianity insists God is personal, while Hinduism believes such a conception would limit his reality. (Impersonality is the more inclusive concept and we must remember that inclusivity has a high value in the East). Now some theologians have tried to reconcile these views. Khin Maung Din indeed tries to have it both ways: God is both personal and impersonal; that is, he is personal but he transcends our ability to describe him (1975:22–23. Perhaps, he notes, "I am what I am" needs this kind of functional definition).

But isn't it also possible to agree that these different conceptions result from fundamentally different experiences? The encounter with a personal God in this case would not be a reflection of (or projection of) Western ideas about personality but a result of a particular kind of religious experience, which in turn has influenced the way we think about the world and even about what it means to be human.

Hideo Ohki, a Japanese theologian, has argued along these lines, saying that in Eastern thought God's transcendence is grounded in human transcendence. The personal intervention of God in Christianity reverses this order. "We cannot reach God via [our] transcendence but rather [our] transcendence as such must be conceived as grounded in God's transcendence" (in Elwood, ed., 1976:152). Ohki goes on to argue that the meaning of this transcendence is not simply the human experience of a depth reality or of the unity of all things; it is God's coming to us from afar, establishing us as persons, what Scripture calls covenant partners (ibid., 155). This encounter, then, not only makes clear what God is like from his side, but defines what our conceptions of a person ought to be. This insight in turn validates, even necesssitates, our interaction with the world, making possible a "history." If our conceptions of history and the self could be shown to rest on this divine initiative, then giving up a sense of particularism, as Song advises, would surely be a step backward and not an advance.

This brings us to the fundamental question Pieris has raised: Can we baptize the ethos of Eastern soteriology as we find it? Another way of phrasing the question would be to ask whether these faiths are really liberative. In the Asian Theological Conference in 1979 Korean theologians intervened to remind the conference that traditional faiths in Asia have not always been liberating, they have not infrequently been oppressive (in Fabella, ed., 1980:168). That is to say, the world as we experience it, even (or especially!) when we experience it deeply and sensitively, is not liberative, it is oppressive. This after all was the first noble truth of Buddha. Moreover, even the suppression of desire does not liberate, for we are still subject to the law of karma.

But I insist again that it is the shape of our experience with God that is decisive. For it is essential to the Christian Gospel that God has come into the world in Christ to bring about a deliverance from bondage (whether to suffering or to the law of karma). As Stephen Neill points out in his discussion of these issues, we must recognize the enormous originality of Christ: "He has called into being a new world of reality" (1976:148). Remember that Sundar Singh recounted that the personal encounter with Christ changed his view about the nature of reality. After comparing Christian and Indian views of God and history, Geoffrey Parrinder concludes, "Christian faith takes on cosmic dimensions when Jesus is considered in relation to historic human life, but as sent by God for our salvation. The doctrine of Christ inescapably involves a new doctrine of God" (1982:265).

As Samuel Rayan has said, Romans 7 is the key to history. For when we have come to see that God has come (from afar) to us in Christ to deliver us from the immanent law to which we were subject, we become aware that we have ourselves been consenting to our bondage. But this sense of sin, which is a personal though not individualistic conception, is not understood until we have seen God as a personal and active agent, seeking us out, not willing that any should perish. When this becomes clear, then we can see ourselves, not as victims of the moral law (punished by our sins, not for them), not merely able to thwart those purposes, but now established as covenant partners, agents who are responsible to take initiative in our world, thus imaging the God who has created and redeemed the earth.

It might be thought that this emphasis on experience with God would undermine our previous insistence on the centrality of Scripture. But as we noted in the introduction, proper use of the authority of Scripture results in the actual lordship of God in our lives (not merely a theoretical confession). The role of Scripture is by the Holy Spirit to bring us to God. It is not difficult to establish the enormous significance of this conception for Asia. Nor is it necessary to see this conception as destroying the religious sensitivities of the region. As Lakshman Wiskremesinghe said during the Sri Lanka conference: "Christians have been able to transmit in Asia commitment to an historical purpose, social service, and community reconstruction to religions preoccupied with an other worldly orientation for incorporation into their total vision of life" (in Fabella, ed., 1980:33).

This is not to say that the Asian worldview will not also have a positive role to play. The total vision of life as a single interconnected whole will have to be corrected. For human sin, God's active intervention and our own responsibility have made their decisive mark on reality: the world is open both to God and to us. But having once established the fact of (and reason for) this discontinuity in reality, the desire for synthesis, so characteristic of Asian thinking, will again have a role to play. For we have noted that the West, in its tendency toward abstraction and analysis, has difficulty seeing things whole. Yet Ephesians 1:10 tells us that God has a plan to "unite [in

Christ] all things, things in heaven and things on earth."
Perhaps, as Rodrigo Tano says, the idea of nonduality will
"provide a clue to viewing reality as a whole" (1983:163).

It should be clear as well how much we have to learn from
a serious encounter with Asian spirituality. Han Chul-Ha of
Korea spoke eloquently of this at the Seoul conference of
evangelical theologians in 1983. When Western theologians
"appropriate biblical revelation to various forms of human
understanding the reality and the power are stripped from God
and his revelation" (1983:35). So Western theology, he believes, dependent as it is on Cartesian rationalism, stands on
human wisdom, not on the power of God. Serious reflection on
the spiritual sensitivities of Asia may help us recover the
spiritual dimension of biblical faith wherein "the spiritual
invisible reality which is directly related to [God] is considered to be more primary than his visible creatures" (ibid.).

A final contribution of Asian thinking, with important
theological as well as missiological implications, may be the
contribution of Buddhist descriptions of the human situation
(see Tano, 1983:163). Human life is marked by change and
decay, and Western theologians, perhaps influenced by exis-
tentialism, are giving more attention to this as a theological
problem. Human suffering immediately raises the question of
God, for as Jürgen Moltmann says, it is not a problem to be
solved, it is "the open wound of life in this world" (1981:47–
48). Filipino Lorenzo Boutista believes that Asian theologians
will make use of the biblical idea of "lament"—the cry of
despair addressed to God, to articulate a genuine faith in God
for a people with histories of protracted suffering (in personal
correspondence). Asian Christians may help us understand
this dimension of life and those parts of Scripture, like the
book of Job, that have puzzled Western interpreters for so long.
Further Asian descriptions of human life in the world may
highlight the biblical picture of human life apart from God,
and, especially, the role, for example, of "spirit" in opening up
this experience to the divine Spirit, as Lynn de Silva has
suggested.

But these insights will not come from Asian thinking in

itself, nor will they come from an encounter between "Christianity" and, say, "Buddhism." They will come only from the actual interaction between Asians grasped by the Gospel and carefully reading the Scriptures and their own Asian setting. But that setting, like all others in the world, will not stay the same after it has experienced the living Lord of history. Thus transformed, it will bring its glory into the heavenly kingdom (see Rev. 21:26).

5

CHRISTOLOGY:
A CROSS-CULTURAL
STUDY

In the preceding chapters I have been arguing that learning about theology from non-Western traditions uncovers dimensions of God's rule that our theologies have sometimes overlooked. If this is true, it would certainly be most apparent in discussions of the person and work of Christ. For Scripture tells us that it was in Christ that God became man, by whose death and resurrection, nature and history have been irrevocably changed. Inevitably, then, the challenge the Gospel brings to all cultures will focus on Christ. What Kwame Bediako says of his African context could be said of all other places as well: "The heart of the encounter of the Good News with our context is Christology; the significance of our faith in Jesus Christ, crucified and risen, for our existence and destiny in the world" (1983A:110).

We might be justified, then, in selecting Christology as a case study to see what shape a cross-cultural study of Christian doctrine might take. But what do we mean by a cross-cultural study of Christ's person and work? Should not Christ make a similar impact on all peoples of the world? After all, isn't Jesus the single Savior of all mankind, the same, the writer of Hebrews puts it, "yesterday, today, and forever" (Heb. 13:8)? Of course this is true and its truth is central to the New Testament. But the New Testament portrays this unity by means of a diversity of images and metaphors. Jesus is presented as the good shepherd (John 10), the representative man (Romans 5), the forerunner (Heb. 6:20), the pioneer (Heb. 2:9–10), the firstfruits from the dead (1 Cor. 15:23), the firstborn of all creation (Col. 1:15), the martyr (Rev. 1:5–6)—to name only a few of the many pictures used.

This variety of imagery has great significance for cross-cultural ministry, for recent research in the New Testament has shown that the various titles, and thus the meanings, given to Christ reflect the various settings in which Jesus was preached and followed. For example, the most common designation of Jesus in the gospels, the Son of Man, disappears almost entirely in Paul's writings. Evidently, whereas the Son of Man—a heavenly figure recalling Daniel 7:13—was perfectly understood among Palestinian Jews, portraying Jesus as "Lord" was more appropriate for Paul's Gentile hearers. But notice that the the different settings resulted in unique theological perspectives. As Stephen Neill observes, "Jerusalem Christians tended to think of Jesus as the one who had gone away into heaven and would one day come again to rejoin his friends . . . whereas Gentile Christians experienced more vividly the presence of the risen Christ through the Holy Spirit in their assemblies" (1976:29).

In one sense, of course, these two expressions—"Son of Man" and "Lord"—say the same thing. But because their context is different, one might say the formulations have to change for the reality to stay the same (see ibid; also James Dunn, 1980). It has become common among biblical scholars to call this circumstantial expression, but what they are really talking about is God's way of contextualizing the Gospel for the first-century audience. John Driver points out that although inspired by the Holy Spirit and thus uniquely authoritative, "the images which appear in the New Testament were most certainly used because they were needed to elucidate the work of Christ in some particular place and some special situation" (1986:31).

But why, then, have we in the West been more interested in the unity than the diversity? Driver, who has spent many years teaching in Latin America, has recently argued that Western theology has gradually replaced the rich imagery of the New Testament with rational formulations of Christ's work. The images of the New Testament, he points out, were pointers, not statements of absolute limits. "Images are pictures of a reality which is bigger than themselves" (ibid., 31). Since the work of God in Christ transcends our human understanding, God has chosen to use a wide range of metaphors that truly portray what Christ was doing. So a certain amount of ambiguity, Driver points out, is necessary to the use of images. But as doctrine has been rationally defined, this imagery has been displaced (we would say explained) by more abstract statements that eliminate ambiguity in the interest of clarity.

It is possible, then, that a dialogue with pictures of Christ from around the world will not only broaden our more narrow conceptions but also restore to us some of the vigor of biblical imagery. In any case the legitimacy of circumstantial expression cannot be doubted by anyone who means to be biblical. As images varied in New Testament times, so the image that becomes important to people today will depend on their setting. My students in North America have always had a hard time understanding why God had to send his Son to die as a blood sacrifice for sins, but they are drawn to images that portray Christ as healing our estrangement from God. Students in Africa, by contrast, have no trouble with the idea of sacrifice, and they readily see Christ's death as placing him in the position of power with reference to God—death being commonly understood this way in Africa.

Since Christ's work is often understood in personal (and even individualistic) terms in the West, there Christ is believed to reign in one's heart. In Africa Christ is the source of God's saving power and so is thought to reign over the world of the spirits. Latin Americans are interested to know how the reign of Christ affects political structures; Asians, by contrast, are interested in biblical images relating to Christ's cosmic reign over the universe. Now these are all biblical images that portray something of Christ's work, but not everyone can relate to all of them. It remains true, however, as we will see, that stretching our minds to think of Christ in different ways will surely illumine parts of Scripture that we have overlooked and, more importantly, will strengthen our faith in the Lord of our own life and history. According to the traditions we have been studying, what is the nature of Christ's union with history and of his saving work?

AFRICA: CHRIST AND THE ANCESTORS

We have seen that for Africans the world is alive with powers that constitute the active agents in the worldview. These powers in fact sustain and uphold the order of things so that any malfunction in the harmony of life is believed to be caused by one or another of these powers and must be remedied by appeal to them. Moreover, beliefs about the powers center on the role of the ancestors as mediators both of the identity and standards of the community and of the power that facilitates its health and happiness. The whole process of birth, circumcision, parenthood, death, and ancestorship is meant to establish and facilitate the flow of power for life. As Cyril Okorocha (1987) has shown, the search for salvation among the Igbo is the quest for power to live a fruitful life.

To the question of how Christ relates to this structure of power two answers have been suggested. The most carefully worked-out view is found in Tanzanian Charles Nyamiti's discussion in his book *Christ as Our Ancestor* (1984). The growth of beliefs about the ancestors, he believes, is a kind of general revelation of God's own way of mediating power. It is a "supernatural imitation and prolongation in men of the Saviour's Brother-Ancestorship toward us" (7). The relations with Christ and with the ancestors have significant differences, of course, but they reflect basic structural similarities that he wants to explore (69). The goal, he says, is to introduce into the African church the traditional piety, adapting it and Christianizing it from within (136).

Nyamiti believes the similarities between Christ's ancestorship and that of our fathers are obvious to any close observer. The authority of both is based on consanguinity (Christ through his Adamite origin, 19), and on their exemplary lives. The authority of both, moreover, is conferred on them by their death. This features the common African tendency to celebrate death, not as an ending, but as the passing to a new level of existence. Kwesi Dickson notes in this connection that all the rites connected with death in Africa have the effect of cementing relationships (in Torres and Fabella, 1978:49; note how similar rites in the West are meant to bring closure to relationships). As the ancestors are thought to be closer to God at their death, so Christ's death confirms his supernatural status (Nyamiti, 29; cf. Eph. 4:9–10).

In both cases the new status both facilitates and requires continuing relationships with those on earth, a fact marked by regular communications—sacrifices and oblations on the one hand and prayer and the Eucharist on the other. Through this continuing relationship these figures become models of conduct and also sources of inner vital power.

Nyamiti is quick to point out, however, that Christ is more than an ancestor. As the God-man, though he affirms blood and race, he transcends them as well (21). As redeemer, prophet, and king he accomplishes more than the ancestors' mediation of power: "For it is through the paschal mystery that He established fully God's kingdom in the charity of the divine spirit" (39–40). And as present through his Holy Spirit he makes possible an actual participation in the divine nature— what the New Testament calls our being sons and daughters of God. In a way that goes beyond any relationship with our ancestors, the goal in our relation with Christ is our becoming like him "through the charity of the divine spirit" (32). Finally, in his resurrection he has begun to gather all his people to himself, the sign of ancestral faithfulness on the part of God the Father. Unlike the Christians of the West, who think of this in individual terms, Nyamiti points out that this resurrection is to be communal, when, one day, the whole Christ will be raised to newness of life (48).

The link with Christ is important, then, not only in bridging the gap to the distant God (who, remember, is thought of as having withdrawn in many African myths) but also in clarifying and purifying our relation with the ancestors. The piety they engender has been placed now in this larger context.

The second model of relating Christ to the ancestors comes from West Africa, specifically the Akan of Ghana. Kwame Bediako is not happy identifying the role of Christ with that of the ancestors (cf. "Biblical Christologies in the Context of African Traditional Religons," 1983A:81–121). He believes one can too easily assume parallels that do not in fact exist. Nor should Christ simply replace the ancestors. "For if the full prerogatives of the Greatest Ancestor are claimed for one who ... does not belong to his clan ... the Akan non-Christian might well feel that the very grounds of his identity and personality are taken away from him" (100). This would seem to the Akan to diminish the role of his real ancestors.

But if Christ must not be shown to discard the social order, he must not be placed in a separate compartment of life either. Surely we must accept Jesus in terms of the cries and pleas of our religious world—we must, says Bediako, make him at home in our religious universe. But the relationship between Christ and the ancestors, Bediako argues, must be thought of in a much more complex and dynamic way than Nyamiti has suggested.

The starting point in reflection on Christ, Bediako insists, is the inclusive dimension of his incarnation (rather than its particularistic aspect). Christ came to establish for all people an "adoptive" past, what he calls the Abrahamic link (101). We are ultimately to find our past as we are assimilated to this story (note the contrast with Aloysius Pieris, who insists that Christianity must be baptized in the Jordan of Eastern faiths, assimilated to their ethos).

But the question remains: How will this relate to the power structure that Africans know? This is accomplished by understanding that Jesus' death heals both the remoteness that we feel from God and the disruption caused by sin. His death has "eternal sacrificial significance for us" (103). But note that his death (and resurrection) has also enthroned Jesus on the "stool of power" with reference to God—Bediako here refers to the enstoolment of the Akan king on the ancestral seat of power (ibid.). From there Christ sends his Holy Spirit and mediates God's saving power.

In sitting on the seat of God's power, Christ does not displace the king, but he does "desacralize" his rule (108). Bediako sees this encounter—between the power of Christ and the supposed saving power of the king, and by extension, of the ancestor—as a power confrontation. In this exchange Christ must pull down strongholds (2 Cor. 10:4–5). The king (or chief) and the ancestors still play an important role in the society, but it now relates to the social solidarity of the people, and not to the mediation of life or of salvation.

In another place Bediako explains why this must happen. In Africa power is dispersed through various agents. Africans see the universe as alive with various levels of power and influence. As power is broadly refracted, so religious activity must be directed in many different directions. In Christianity, while the existence of various kinds of power is recognized, God's saving power is focused on Christ (Col. 1:15–20; Gitari and Benson, 1986:85) "Christ assumes the roles of all these points of our piety which we addressed . . . to various sources of power" (Bediako, 1983A:117).

Both Nyamiti and Bediako are working in terms of the African worldview. But they work with it in very different ways. Nyamiti wants to work from within outward, Christianizing the traditional piety; Bediako works in a dynamic interaction between the traditional piety and the coming of Christ, as the latter displaces the former in respect to the mediation of power. As Bediako graphically describes this, "Once Christ has come the ancestors are cut off as the means of blessing for we lay our power lines differently" (ibid., 115).

The contrast between these two approaches may be summarized in the words *christianization* and *desacralization*. Nyamiti wants to assimilate African piety within his Christian framework, whereas Bediako wants to desacralize this piety, without losing the continuing role of the traditional order. This is very important, for Bediako insists that the questions of identity and social organization are crucial, and the structure that supports these should be maintained. But religious allegiance lies elsewhere. This desacralization recalls what happened at the Reformation, when the world was liberated from the powers, and thus under God became the arena for God's people to exercise their freedom. Exploration, science, and commerce were thus encouraged. In the summary to this chapter, pages 180–84, we will inquire into whether Christianity cannot play a similar role in many parts of the Third World today.

LATIN AMERICA: CHRIST AND POLITICAL POWER

The Latin American world raises for its people a wholly different set of questions with which it approaches the person of Christ. As we saw, this is conditioned by a special and painful reading of history. Latin America has been the scene of centuries of economic and cultural invasion by political powers that have left this people with a lingering sense of powerlessness. This widely accepted sense of living on the underside of history has given rise to special questions about Christ.

The first set of questions relates to what the conquering powers have made of Christ. Latin American theologians have, in the words of René Padilla, felt an urgent need to "examine the images of Jesus Christ with which traditional Christianity has generally been associated and which have often served as the basis for Christian mission" (Samuel and Sugden, 1983:12). Jon Sobrino, whose views we will examine in some detail, wonders whether the abstract Christ, the imperial Christ, or the power-wielding Christ have not been used in Latin America to maintain the status quo (1978:xvi–xix). In another place he traces the origin of liberation Christology to "an expression of indignation over the use to which Christ has so often been put in the history of Latin America in order to justify the oppression of the poor" (1987:12).

The second concern is the reverse of this. If Christ has been sometimes "domesticated" by Western theology, what would it look like to reread his life from the point of view of the poor? If Christ has been imprisoned by other interests, how can he now be made accessible to those who have been excluded from this reading? As Leonardo Boff said at the beginning of his controversial study of Christology: "It is with preoccupations that are ours alone, taken from our Latin American context that we will reread not only the old texts of the New Testament but also the most recent commentaries written in Europe" (1978:43).

Latin theologians admit that they too bring interests to the text—there is no privileged reading. Boff describes these interests as human-centered rather than church-centered, utopian rather than factual, critical rather than dogmatic, with concern for orthopraxis rather than orthodoxy (ibid., 44–47). Sobrino begins with the concrete life of Jesus, described in the light of the Latin American context. Both men want to move between the poles of the concrete life of Jesus and their situation (Sobrino, 1978:2, 13) so that they can make their praxis of liberation—remember this is the theological starting point in Lating America—more critically minded (ibid., 33).

This leads them naturally to a Christology that takes history, their own and Christ's, seriously. Because their history brings them to see their situation, not as needing explanation, but as demanding transformation, they feel that it is within history that answers must be found. It follows then, Sobrino believes, that the only proper way of comprehending Jesus is through his historical life. This is shown, as we might expect, by the fact that when the church started from the other end—that is, from dogma about Christ—it made Christ into an alienating force (ibid., 315, 353) [the following unmarked references are from this source]. But even more importantly we begin with Jesus' story, because Jesus himself insisted that his actual life was the locus of God's liberating work. Since we are concerned with the actual transformation of our sistuation, we are after a discipleship that reflects Jesus' life and thus collaborates in his liberating work (35).

When we examine his life, we find that it focused on the arrival of the kingdom of God (41), which is a "restructuring of visible, tangible relationships existing between human beings" (44). The importance of this lies in two directions. In the first place, Sobrino believes the actual practice of his relationships with the Father (and other people) constitutes the essence of his person. He actually demonstrates his sonship—he even becomes son—through his work of bringing in the kingdom (105–7). Sobrino puts the matter in such stark terms because he wants to define Jesus' sonship relationally rather than essentially. Unlike African theologians, who define sonship in terms of descent and likeness, Sobrino insists it is revealed in the course of Jesus' surrender to the Father over the course of his life on earth (268).

But this has significance for a second reason. From our point of view, only in following Jesus do we understand what our sonship is. Only in the practice of obedience "do we glimpse the mental categories that will enable us to 'understand' the kingdom" (60). Moral theology (ethics) focuses, then, on what must be done to establish the kingdom of God in history (113). Indeed, being human can be defined as participating in God's process, which quite literally is the divine life (234).

The Cross and the Resurrection, then, can be understood as the consequence of this historical life. A focus on theories of the Atonement, Sobrino believes, hides the real scandal, that "the cross was the historical consequence of his life, the process whereby Jesus *becomes the son* through his concrete history" (201, his emphasis. cf. 214). Similarly the Resurrection is the promise of God's power over injustice and even death. God is the power of deliverance not in the abstract but in the contrete (276–77). Experience of this resurrection makes us truly "ec-centric" and our lives truly an "ex-odus," lived for others as a liberating presence (264).

This approach to Christ emphasizes that for us meaning is discovered only as we follow him in recreating justice (122). The Spirit of Jesus always prompts a re-creation of Jesus' human history in us, incorporating us into the process of God himself, a process that was seen in Jesus' life (138, 226). There is no access to this God apart from living in a way that corresponds to his love, and this means that we know God, not directly, or mystically, but indirectly through service to the poor (277).

Sobrino admits that dogmas about Christ are important. We must end there, but that is not where we begin. Ontologically we know the Son became man, but epistemologically we begin at the other end (339). Dogmas formulate boundaries, but they are the end of a process of reflection, not the point of departure for discipleship. For what Christ came to do was not to reveal the Father's essense but to demonstrate the way one must respond to God (387–8). Chalcedon is true, but only as long as there are followers whose discipleship actually reflects it! (342).

In many ways the Latin American reflection on Christ is a refreshing plea for a return to Christ's original call to discipleship. It reminds us that Christ came into the world to change us into his image, not merely to teach us truths about God— though it would be a mistake to dichomotize these. Moreover there is in the New Testament (and in its Hebrew background generally) a functionalist strand that is apparent, for example, in Romans 1:4: "Through the Spirit of holiness [Christ] was declared with power to be the Son of God by his resurrection from the dead."

It seems clear that in the New Testament believers began their reflection on Christ by experiencing his deliverance and new life. They experienced his death and resurrection before they understood it (cf. Driver, 1986:15; Klaas Runia, 1984:96). But it is equally clear that this work of Christ was immediately connected, in their minds, to his person. For "action implies prior being—even if it is also true, being is only apprehended in action" (R. H. Fuller, quoted in ibid.). Even if one starts with the effects of Christ's work, one is promptly faced with the question of his divine character. We will want to return to this question further on.

But having said this, I must acknowledge that Latin American theology is probing one of the most sensitive areas of biblical Christology: In what ways does Jesus' humanity imply a growth in understanding and a learning through obedience (Luke 1:80; Heb. 5:8)? How might the admission of such growth affect our discipleship? Does it contradict statements regarding Jesus' preexistence? René Padilla insisted at the 1982 Conference of Evangelical Missions' Theologians that the real problem is that "we live in a world where dogma prevails" (in Samuel and Sugden, 1983:31). We therefore find it difficult to identify ourselves imaginatively with the historical Jesus as he lived among the poor. If we were able to do this, it might not seem so shocking to us to realize that there was a political dimension to Jesus' life and to his teaching about the kingdom. Perhaps this fondness for abstraction accounts not only for dogmatic Christology, Padilla goes on to suggest, but also for the rise of Marian traditions in Latin America. Perhaps Christological dogmas were so pale and distant that people created in Mary a mother who loves them and stays close to them (ibid.). Can we learn from this and portray a Savior who walks the way we walk and understands our weaknesses?

But in their Latin eagerness to bring Christ down to a human level, there is a danger that they will minimize his present role at the right hand of God—which African theologians emphasized. There are two problems that we may note here. One is that insistence on the historical life of Jesus, at least as this is portrayed in the New Testament, provides no refuge from dogma. Boff and Sobrino both know that the Gospels give no access to Christ's life apart from a theological interpretation. Boff takes this as simply the indication that "Christ is constituted as the meeting point of religious hermeneutics, of the history of the world and human beings" (1978:43). He believes that this does not hinder Latin Americans from taking him as their starting point "as people touched by the significance of his reality" (ibid.). One might say in their defense, as Christine Gudorf has done, that liberation theology has its own "Christ of Faith"; they simply put flesh on the bones at different points (1987:11). This may be so, but at least there needs to be more honesty in admitting the role of dogma in interpreting Christ's historical life.

The second problem is that the New Testament interpretation of Christ as divine Lord does not diminish the role that Jesus' historical life can play for the Christian, but rather enhances it. It was precisely, Paul tells us, because Jesus did not cling to the prerogatives of divinity but took on the role of servant, that he was given a name that is above every name. This requires every knee to bow but it also asks that we have in ourselves the same mind, which looks not only after our own things (Phil. 2:5–10). It is what we might call the "divine context" of Christ's life that gives it its full meaning and, we might add, its saving quality. For as René Padilla notes, "Unless the death of Christ is also seen as God's gracious provision of an atonement for sin, the basis for forgiveness is removed and sinners are left without the hope of justification" (Samuel and Sugden, 1983:28).

This larger context has implications for our discipleship as well. We have appreciated at various points the emphasis of liberation theology on the necessity of particular practice in order for corresponding truths to be known. But the New Testament is also clear that a life of righteousness is not possible by unaided human efforts. The larger suprahistorical context of Jesus' life reminds us that the kingdom not only comes to us as demand, it is also a gift of God, demonstrated and effected by the pouring out of the Holy Spirit. Jesus did not come to the world only to become a son through obedience, but also to bring from heaven the messianic kingdom. He told the Pharisees, "If I drive out demons by the Spirit of God, then the kingdom of God has come upon you" (Matt. 12:28).

As African theologians reminded us, it is our experience of the kingdom, the grace of sonship, that is Christ's greatest gift. So Charles Nyamiti could say, "It is hoped that African theology will contribute to restore once again the primordial importance of the grace of sonship in all Christian efforts" (1984:50).

ASIA: CHRIST AND THE TRANSCENDENT

It is hard to imagine two more different approaches to Christ than those of Latin America and Asia. Whereas one insists on starting and meditating on the historical life of Jesus, the other finds such a procedure positively distasteful. Remember that for the Asian the events of history, as for the Greeks, are a secondary and deceptive reality. How can salvation depend on such events?

Burmese theologian Khin Muang Din illustrates this difficulty well. His starting point is typical of Asian theology: the Gospel must be universal, so it must be expressed in truly universal categories. But to insist, then, on the particularities of Jesus' life is to introduce an unnecessary stumbling block. One cannot deny the raw fact of Jesus, "but," says Din, "I question the authenticity of universalizing him from a purely Jewish context. . . . To formulate a more relevant Christology for today we must be able to distinguish the particularity and temporality of the Jesus event from the universality and eternality of the Christ event in the ongoing process of universal history" (1975:25). Whereas the former interested Latin theologians, the latter grabs the attention of Asians. They want to know: How does this universal Christ deliver from the bondage to the law of karma? Behind this there looms the larger question: What finally is the relation between this Christ and that Jesus?

To illustrate the Asian approach to Christ we study the work of S. J. Samartha entitled *The Hindu Response to the Unbound Christ* (1974, excerpted in Elwood, ed., 1976:221–39). Samartha begins with the obvious positive response of Hindus to Christ and wonders whether the principle of advaida might be a means of communicating a deeper reality of Christ to them. ("Advaita," from the eighth-century Hindu philosopher Sankara, refers to non-duality, or at-one-ness, which draws together God, the world, and people in a single conception.)

With this starting point Samartha asks, "What is the reality that one encounters in Jesus of Nazareth as the living and risen Lord, in the totality of his life, death and resurrection, and how, through him, [is] a renewal of human life possible?" (in Elwood, 223). Like Latin American theologians, Samartha has trouble expressing this in the two-nature language of Chalcedon. But their unease with this formulation reflects two very different settings. Whereas Sobrino found the formula too abstract and distant, Samartha believes it is too limiting! Latin Americans seek to maintain the radically historical character of theology; Asians by contrast, work in a metaphysical framework that makes it difficult for them to comprehend personhood in terms of localized interiority (225).

But Samartha is not content to simply identify Christ as an *advaitin*—that is, one who has realized his identity with the Brahman—for the social and historical dimensions of Christ's work must be taken seriously. In a previous chapter we noticed how seriously Samartha wants to take the impact of the Gospel. It is interesting that he quotes Oscar Cullmann and notes, with apparent approval, this theologian's insistence that salvation history is essential to understanding Christ's deity (228). Christ does more than simply realize his own "divinity"; he brings salvation. Moreover, he introduces into history the pull of purpose: a kingdom that allows creation of the new, not merely a realization of the old (230–31).

The New Testament does hold out an important gathering-together role for Christ at the end of history (Eph. 1:10). So Samartha is right in stressing, "As the agent of creation and as the savior of mankind, [Christ's] work is continuing until all things are summed up in him" (231). But there is uniqueness to this work of Christ that cannot be accounted for in vague Hindu aspirations toward a final union of all reality. On the one hand, Christ's future guarantees the freedom and responsibility of the person toward this world; it values the historical and social dimensions of life. But on the other hand, it will be a new creation, something that comes down out of heaven! (231).

So Christ has introduced to human experience a new dimension that makes possible the emergence of something new in history. His death and resurrection provide "the inspiration and power to a life of service, of suffering and victory . . . [so that] wherever the Christ-event is recognized, and wherever people are consciously prepared to die with him and to be raised with him, there God's work of reconciliation takes place" (235–36). Christ's suffering completely transcends all Hindu thinking on the subject. For the Hindu it is not possible for one to suffer for the sins of others—to do so would upset the whole system of justice (as Tagore pointed out; 233).

But the problem that we encountered in our earlier discussion of Asian theology emerges again: What does it mean to recognize the Christ-event in our experience? And, more importantly, what connection does this event have with the life of Jesus of Nazareth? Some Asians seem to recognize him in the spirituality of the people and in their quest for deliverance (Aloysius Pieris); others see him present in the struggles of Asians to live a human life (Choan-Seng Song). The latter view virtually identifies the Incarnation with the suffering and striving of Asians. "The truth of the Christian Faith has as its fulcrum the word becoming flesh, God becoming a human person, the divine becoming human, the life and history of God becoming the life and history of human beings" (Song, 1984:9).

As Latin Americans have forced us to ask about the meaning of Jesus the man for the oppressed of Latin America, Asians insist that we consider the larger cosmic dimensions of Christ's work. They force us to consider the final goal toward which creation moves—a good that will be "an enrichment and a fulfillment, moving through struggles and conflicts, overcoming evil in love, gathering up values, reaching out, and finding fulfillment in the fulness of God" (Samartha in Elwood, 237). But as Latins are tempted to see Jesus' actions in all struggles for justice, so Asians see there the sign of the final consummation. Samartha is aware of the difficulties this raises, for he insists that while Christ is involved in struggles for justice, he is not bound by them (238).

But precisely how, then, is one to know where Christ is working? Western Christians have taken what we might call the minimalist approach: Christ is working among people who call on him and where his word is preached. As Vinay Samuel and Chris Sugden have pointed out, these specifications have limited God's presence to those who accept a right system of doctrine; such people have not been able to think historically (or we might add "incarnationally") about Christ's presence (Samuel and Sugden, 1983:139). But Asian theologians have gone to the other extreme, taking what we might call the maximalist approach: Christ is present everywhere a person seeks liberation in the transcendent or struggles to live a human life.

Samartha is not comfortable with these alternatives. He does not want to unbind Christ from Western culture only to bind him again to this Hindu context. He wants to take seriously the historical and social situation. But how does one do this? A start has to be made by taking the facts of Christ's life and death as presented in the New Testament as nonnegotiable. Much as Khin Muang Din dislikes it, it is the raw fact of Christ that is the bridge between God and humanity (cf. Sumithra and Nicholls, 1983:179). This is the stress of Latin American theologians and it is sorely needed in Asia. The fulcrum that Song seeks in the word's becoming flesh is irrevocably connected to those central events of Jesus' life and death. Indeed it was his death, African theologians insist, that has placed him in a position of power with respect to God. This event has given him the leverage necessary to communicate deliverance.

Still Asian theologians press us to ask questions that are harder to answer: The nonviolent revolution of Ghandi, was it of God or of Satan? Or was it a matter of indifference to God? These questions press upon one and relate to the final goal toward which history moves. Here perhaps the monistic framework of Asian thinkers proves a handicap in the hard work of discernment. For the kingdom is not simply an evolutionary climax (this would be, as Samartha admits, merely the realization of the old), but it is the appearance of the new, coming down out of heaven from God. And this new thing, which has made its appearance in Christ's life and death, is radically contested in this historical period, Scripture says, by the power of evil. Just as it has proven difficult for Asians to attribute saving significance to the particular events of Christ's life, so it is proving difficult to locate particular present events that are signs of this coming new world.

SUMMARY

This brief review of Christological thinking has certainly demonstrated the diversity of imagery that Christ's work has called forth around the world. How do we evaluate this discussion? Is there no limit to the range of christologies possible? How does Scripture interact with these conversations? Before turning to these questions, however, it is appropriate to note the common themes that characterize thinking about Christ in the Third World and that distinguish it from Western studies of Christ.

All three discussions we have surveyed agree that Christ must be understood in functional terms. Christ has come into the world to bring salvation. Although this has been defined variously by different theologians, all are more interested in what Christ has done and will do than in understanding precisely who he is. All seek a power in him: power for a full life, power to follow Jesus in his concern for the poor, power for release from the cosmic law. Consequently all three focus more on his work than on his person. When his person is thought of at all, Third World theologians, in contrast to Western theologians, conceive of it relationally and communally rather than individualistically (e.g., with concern about defining his divine-human nature). While this has given a new relevance to the work of Christ, we need to ask whether this concern with function has not carried certain risks.

Nevertheless, it is clear that each area has made a unique contribution and raised urgent questions that Christological discussions should now consider. Africans urge us to see the communal and cultural signficance of sonship and the rule of Christ at God's right hand; Latin Americans remind us that Christ's lordship must be reflected in concrete human contests with the political powers; Asians push us further and ask how Christ's transcendent lordship relates to our human struggles.

In their concluding statement the evangelical mission theologians meeting in Thailand in 1982 sought to bring these questions together: Christology, they said, must

> stress the historical reality, the man of Nazareth in Galilee in his concrete socioeconomic, political, racial and religious context. This Jesus is also the incarnate Word of God . . . we affirm the universal lordship of Jesus Christ. A full Christology must include both these understandings and one aspect cannot be stressed without reference to the other. (Samuel and Sugden, 1983:278)

In many ways our few examples have demonstrated the wisdom of this statement. For in almost every case a proper concern with the urgencies of the context has threatened to separate the historical life and work of Jesus from his role as universal Lord. In the theologies of Asia and Africa the events of his historical life are, for different reasons, not given any major significance. In Latin America, by contrast, the historical life of Christ is sometimes abstracted from—or even substituted for—its larger setting in the universal reign of God the Father.

This might in part be excused by noting that these are rough and undeveloped statements, making up in freshness for what they lack in depth. And one must recall the historical dynamic that we have seen working in the evolution of Third World thought. Most Christological thinking in the Third World accepts as axiomatic that reflection on Christ must be done in the light of local realities. At the same time, experience with Christ in one place (usually they are thinking of the West) must not be made normative elsewhere. All such discussions make severe judgments about such "spiritual imperialism." To some extent such reminders are helpful.

But the solution to such domination is certainly not "spiritual parochialism." Even a sympathetic observer is struck by the fact that tendencies to emphasize the historical Jesus or the power of the ancestral or cosmic Christ, however well intentioned and relevant, can easily lead to oversimplification and misunderstanding. An emphasis on the function and power of Christ is important and necessary, but this must be matched by a recognition of the theological realities that underlie these effects. Christ delivers us from bondage precisely because eternally he shares the being of God and expresses his divinity and his redemptive victory in the pouring out of the Holy Spirit.

This issue of theological strategy, however, leads to a further issue: The concern to reflect theologically on the various settings has not by and large been matched by an equal concern to apply the realities of Scripture—or the resources of Christian tradition—to that setting. In the present discussion this weakness is evident in the failure to locate discussions of Christ in the larger biblical and Trinitarian context of his life and work. As a rule, interaction with Scripture, or even with the Christian tradition, has not been profound. Jon Sobrino may not unfairly be taken as an example. In many ways he does more than many to deepen the discussion; his comments on Jesus' relation to the Father in the context of his humanity are very important and are supported by lengthy and perceptive exegetical discussions. But there are significant lacunae. In one of only two references I found to the Holy Spirit he says:

> In God himself the Spirit is the fruit of the love between Father and Son, as tradition tells us. In history, however, this love takes a historical form: It becomes the spirit of love designed to effect liberation in history. (1978:226)

Understanding God as such a "process" of love, he goes on to say, enables us to see Christian existence as a "way"—and ourselves as coactors in history (ibid., see also 1987:51–53, where he explains that "God is a trinitarian process").

But tradition, or in this case Augustine, would certainly not simply affirm the notion that God is a Trinitarian process. This in fact is an idea that has appeared only recently and has been developed most fully by German theologian Jürgen Moltmann—though, to be sure, in dialogue with theologians in the Third World. Now it is true that taking history with greater seriousness theologically, as we have tended to do in our century, may in the end prove an important advance. But we can only discover this by engaging in a deeper dialogue with Scripture and other traditions in a much more self-critical manner than is evident in the discussions we have reviewed.

In general it is easier to dismiss previous conversations about Christ as irrelevant (or ideologically tainted) than it is to enter into serious interaction with them. Indeed, there is a certain irony in dismissing traditional theology as Western, for the Christological formulations culminating in Chalcedon emerged out of long conversations between Western theologians, who had at least some contact with Africa (cf. Cyprian and Augustine), and those from the East (like Origen), who were deeply influenced by oriental modes of thinking. Other traditions have continued to make their impact on theology—one thinks of the Eastern Orthodox Church in our own century—though not perhaps in the magnitude they promise to do in the future.

But as these fresh essays in Christology from the Third World may be flawed by insufficient interaction with tradition and Scripture, we must not, for our part, underestimate the contribution that they have to make. Sometimes an encounter with a variety of traditions leads to a fear that the faith once delivered to the saints may be seriously distorted, or even lost. Such dangers of course are very real. But my remarks at the beginning of the chapter should have made clear that contemporary discussions of Christology and studies of the New Testament are opening up new ways of examining issues. The faith about Christ, far from being fixed, is being reexamined in new and exciting ways. As Klaas Runia notes, the formulation of Chalcedon has not closed discussion.

Let us consider briefly a few of the issues that call for fresh discussion. First, while it is clear that the nature of Christ and his mission of salvation are inseparable, it is not clear how these are to be related (Runia, 1984:105). Second, the exact nature of the Incarnation is receiving new and important attention. While this has traditionally been expressed in substantialist categories, these categories are becoming increasingly unsatisfactory. A contemporary Catholic theologian has reopened the discussion by proposing that we understand the Incarnation relationally as the fulfillment of the covenant between God and man. "The relational being of the Son of God has penetrated humanity as a dynamic principle of transformation. We must visualize the Incarnation in this essentially dynamic perspective" (Jean Galot, 1981:75). Third, these very discussions can signal an imbalanced emphasis on the Incarnation over against the Resurrection. It is clearly the latter event that serves as the starting point of apostolic discussions of Christ (cf. Dunn, 1980:267–68). This suggests that somehow the approach "from above" and that "from below" be related from the very beginning. But again the question is how are they related?

These are open questions that call for response from all who follow Christ and love his word. It would be foolish to assume that fresh insight may not come as easily from some of the thinkers we have surveyed as from those in the West.

Clearly the younger churches are asking questions of the tradition and forcing considerations of dimensions of human experience that promise to greatly enrich the theology of the next generation. Indeed the fact that each of the three areas of the world has stressed a different dimension of Christ's work reminds us that a proper reading of Scripture must be made by the whole body of Christ. For Christ himself reminded the disciples just before his ascension: "All authority in heaven and on earth has been given to me" (Matt. 28:18), and Paul insists that every knee will bow before him "in heaven and on earth and under the earth" (Phil. 2:10). Clearly the extent of this reign needs the experience of all his people and the whole of history (and eternity) to fathom.

6

WHERE DO WE GO FROM HERE?

Pity this busy monster, manunkind,

not. Progress is a comfortable disease:
your victim (death and life safely beyond)
plays with the bigness of his littleness
—electrons deify one razorblade
into a moutainrange; lenses extend
unwish through curving wherewhen till unwish
returns on its unself.
          A world of made
is not a world of born—pity poor flesh
and trees, poor stars and stones, but never this
fine specimens of hypermagical
ultraomnipotence. We doctors know
a hopeless case if—listen: there's a hell
of a good universe next door; let's go.

                              e. e. cummings

WHO SEES THINGS WHOLE?

People naturally assume the superiority of their own way of doing things. The encounter with other traditions surely teaches us to see the limitations of our own point of view. Of course there is nothing necessarily perverse about a limited perspective. This restriction, after all, reflects the particularity of our own situation, and it is this situation that is to be the arena for our discipleship. It has become popular these days to urge people to become "world Christians." Much of this is good if it encourages us to raise our eyes beyond our narrow interests and reflect on God's concern for the whole world. But the fact remains that we are not called to minister to the whole world. Our calling is much more modest: to minister to a particular people in their special setting.

Our interest in other traditions may lead us to seek ministry elsewhere—we should always be open to God's call. But its first work is to help us reflect more deeply on our own setting, to the end that our witness there may be more effective. Our primary concern, then, in this conclusion is to inquire what we in the West can learn from Third World theology and, in a more tentative fashion, what they might be able to learn from us.

In general it has become clear that the different emphases of various regions have been mutually illuminating—now complementing, occasionally at odds with one another. This is as it should be if discipleship is meant to be rooted in its setting. While Africa has led the way in examining the close interrelation between cultural patterns and the Gospel, it has tended (except in the South) to overlook the importance of political and economic structures. The Latin American theologians, on the other hand, were keenly interested in the way the Gospel impacted these structures so much so that one could almost say they tended to overvalue the political and historical dimensions of life. Hardly any thought was given to the transcendent world and the new heaven and new earth— indeed, their unique history has made them suspicious of this aspect of theology because it has so often been used to reinforce oppressive structures. In Asia, by contrast, one can almost say religion amounted to a quest for union with the transcendent dimension of life. This was often accompanied by a disparagement of the historical and social realities of life as ultimately illusory. Needless to say, much is to be gained by a serious interchange between these points of view.

We observed in the introduction that all our knowledge today inevitably has a cross-cultural character (cf. Benjamin Nelson, 1981). If this is true of politics and science, it ought certainly to be true of theology. Our discussion of Christology provided a case study of the shape a cross-cultural study in theology might take. Let us take one further example here. We have seen how limited an understanding of poverty is to be had by one group of people. Latin Americans saw poverty in its economic and political dimensions. Indeed, they have done more than others to put poverty on the theological agenda. But their political bias made them blind to the more positive, spiritual values that poverty may exhibit. Here Asians have been able to take us further by incorporating the Latin American perspective on unjust poverty into a larger framework in which voluntary poverty may play a positive role.

But we should quickly add that parochial points of view do not reside only in the Third World. Our Western blind spots are even more gaping—among them, at least until recently, the very existence of poverty as a serious problem in the West. Paul Hiebert gives an example of our myopia in his 1982 article "The Flaw of the Excluded Middle." He noted that most missionaries reflected their Western training by thinking on only two levels: Above, God rules and is concerned with the eternal destiny of people; below, matter operates according to scientific laws. Not only do these two realms operate according to different models (organic or personal on the one hand, and impersonal and mechanistic on the other), but their interrelation is only vaguely understood. I have participated in theological arguments in North America where we have tried to determine how far down the scale God's interest goes before the reign of natural law takes over—clearly we should pray for a job if we are unemployed, but should we pray for a parking place when we are late to a meeting?

As a result, when people like Venkayya, whom we discussed in the introduction, come to missionaries to ask how the spirits and ancestors may be appeased, the missionaries have no answers—that realm simply does not exist for them. The middle level of powers that mediates between God and the material world is excluded. It is little wonder that Westerners have trouble "integrating" their secular and spiritual lives or that missions has been one of the major secularizing forces in modern history. Here is one obvious place where a conscious interaction between worldviews is urgently needed. As Paul

Hiebert concludes, "Only as human history is placed within a cosmic framework does it take on meaning, and only when history has meaning does human biography become meaningful" (ibid., 46).

In many ways this illustrates the central problem arising from our study of Third World theologies. We might put it in the form of this question: How do those seeking to come to terms with the modern world learn to understand and control the world without losing the sense of God's presence? Or, conversely, how do the possessors of power in this world regain their role as God's stewards?

These pointed questions ought to remind us that interchange between cultures is not a simple and pleasant exchange of views. It is certainly not simple and it may well be unpleasant, for gaining insight into our blindspots is never easy, as it tends to multiply, not reduce, our uncertainties. But, as Clifford Geertz says, growth comes only at the cost of inward ease (1983:45).

THE THIRD WORLD AND RENEWAL

We have noted at several points that theology in the Third World is often functional in character. Whereas we in the West are interested in the nature and meaning of reality—witness our theological preoccupation with the "nature of God" or the "nature of the person"—Third World Christians are concerned with its operation. Once after I had given comprehensive lectures on categories of African worldviews, my African students covered the same material in their reports by considering how these things actually work for Africans. Their stories elicited far more discussion (and learning) than my outline! I was interested in defining these concepts; they wanted to know what the corresponding realities actually achieved.

The concrete orientation of this theological reflection relates in part to the urgencies of the issues facing Christians of the younger churches. This same quality gives Third World theology a lay, everyday-life orientation that is most refreshing. Scripture and Christian teaching are brought to bear on issues of immediate concern to the people, usually by those whose theological education, by Western standards, would be considered limited. This has stimulated the idea, especially in Latin America, that educated leaders must learn to take their cues from the Christian community as a whole. Gustavo Gutiérrez has gone so far as to call for the "death of the professional theologian" (Torres and Fabella, 1978:195).

This down-to-earth outlook is reflected in a further fact: Third World theology is ordinarily a theology of mission, or at least a theology done in terms of mission. Here missiologist Johannes Verkuyl is on target:

> It goes without saying that African theology does all the things which theology does in general, but in African Theology (as in Asia) all these other functions are embraced in the missionary or communicative function. It is not primarily an intra-ecclesiastical exercise, but a discipline whose practitioners keep one question central: How can we best do our theology so that the Gospel will touch Africans most deeply? (1978:277)

Professor Verkuyl, who spent many years as a missionary in Africa, is making this as an empirical observation rather than a normative judgment. In general, thinkers in the Third World do their work "on the run" while engaged in a busy life of ministry—problems are so pressing and urgent that long reflection is a luxury most of them cannot afford.

All of this of course recalls the way Paul did his theology in the New Testament. One can readily imagine him dashing off a letter, probably containing deep theological insight, between meetings on a missionary journey. In fact I have heard New Testament scholar Chester Wood argue that the most exalted theological treatise in the New Testament, Romans, was written as an integral part of Paul's missiological strategy: he wanted to make Rome a center of missionary outreach into Spain, as Jerusalem had been a center of outreach earlier (cf. Rom. 15:22–24).

This missionary orientation, Walbert Buhlmann has argued, has major significance for the church around the world.

In reviewing the history of the church, he concludes that "what precisely enabled the church to overcome its periods of low ebb and its times of bitter dissension has been its constantly renewed commitment to the missionary enterprise" (1977:8). He argues, in fact, that the link between renewal and missions is causal: renewal takes place on account of mission.

IS THE WEST AT THE END OF ITS HISTORY?

Few would argue that Christianity, especially in Europe, is not in serious need of renewal. Indeed the sense of fatigue and ending is pervasive in much of the literature and art of the West. Lesslie Newbigin has recently argued that Western civilization is at the point of having lost its hope in the future (1983). The culture of modernity, which began at the Enlightenment, has for many people reached the end of its resources. During that great intellectual earthquake of two hundred years ago, natural explanations replaced theological ones and the interests of the autonomous individual replaced those of the community. As a result, economic growth came almost to be equated with the advance of the kingdom of God. Now we are at the point where our reason no longer explains anything and so-called economic progress is excluding an increasingly large percentage of the human race.

By contrast the Third World, in spite of its enormous problems, still is able to muster considerable hope for the future. Anyone who has spent any time in the Third World becomes deeply impressed with the personal and community resources that can be mobilized to cope with crises and impressed no less deeply with the spirit of hope that pervades these efforts. Recently we received a Christmas letter from a Filipina friend who noted, in spite of the challenges facing her country, how exciting it is to live in a place where history seems to be just beginning, rather than coming to an end as it seems to be in the West.

What role has Christianity played in this Western crisis of faith? Originally, we will note, it had been one of the factors in the rise of science. But since the Enlightenment, not only has it lost its critical edge and its role as salt and light, but it appears to many to have made serious compromises with the spirit of the age. Lesslie Newbigin argues that Christianity is in an advanced state of syncretism (1983:20).

Evidence for this is not hard to find. Theologian David Tracy of the University of Chicago, for example, believes the great modern experiment of freedom is the Enlightenment's bequest to the modern era, an experiment characterized by a "demand for freedom from oppressive authorities and freedom for autonomous, critical, rational thought" (1975:4–5). This tradition is embodied in what he calls the "classics," which comprise the canon of great literature. These writings contain perceptions that have become normative for the whole world and have issued in a widely shared secular faith in liberation. Ironically he faults liberation theologians for trying to maintain faith in the living God of theism and his revelation of himself in Scriptures. This outdated faith in an all-knowing God and exclusivist views of revelation, he believes, "threatens the ultimate value and meaning of the basis of secular faith shared by all those committed to the contemporary struggle for liberation" (ibid., 245; cf. discussion of this in Gudorf, 1987:13). Notice how the Gospel, which G. K. Chesterton called that great blow against the backbone of history and which introduced the concepts of freedom and liberation into the Western vocabulary, is now accused of threatening the secular mission of liberation.

Clearly this line of reasoning does not display any great willingness on the part of Western theologians to listen to what theologians from other regions are saying. It appears that Tracy, along with many others in the West, is unable to hear anyone else over the noise of this "enlightenment project." Newbigin argues that what is necessary is a fresh missionary encounter between the Gospel and Western culture (1983:47; he does a great deal to foster this encounter in his own later book *Foolishness to the Greeks*, 1986). If what I am saying is true, such a renewal in mission may well be a prerequisite to renewal in theological reflection in the West.

THE THIRD WORLD AND MODERNIZATION: WHAT ROLE WILL THEOLOGY PLAY?

While the secular project is worshiped in the West, it is very often maligned in the Third World. In fact all the theologies we have studied (with the notable exception of that of the Philippines) could be characterized in Peter Berger's terms, as countermodernizing ideologies. In his ground-breaking work *The Homeless Mind* (1973), he and his colleagues seek to define the cognitive dimension of the process of modernization. They point out that certain thinking patterns have grown up as the reflection of technologically induced economic growth: rationality and measurability, anonymous social relations and the dichotomization of private and public life, and the separability of means and ends (1973:9ff.).

This way of thinking has become a part of the Western worldview, and it is being exported, along with development programs and computers, to the Third World. Although initially welcomed, this process is being met with increasing misgiving and outright opposition, especially on the part of the educated elite of the Third World. Opposition often takes the form of a resurgence of nationalism and a reassertion of traditional values, what Berger calls counter-modernizing influences. The role of Christianity in all this has been extremely complex, not to say controversial. For in the first instance missionaries were the carriers of this modern consciousness. But now the Christians engaged in theological reflection, usually first-or second-generation Christians, stand in uneasy relationship both to their missionary teachers and the modernization they brought.

Much of their reaction is a healthy recovery of indigenous values and, more importantly, of a dignity that will allow local intitiative. But some of it ignores the inevitable influence modern values have had on their own thinking. As Berger points out, "Almost any contact between different cognitive systems leads to mutual contamination" (ibid., 165). Indeed one can be countermodernizing only by employing modern ideas! Clearly the worldwide process of modernization in

192

economics, in communication and transportation, and even in fashion has become virtually irreversible. We cannot throw these modern packages out—we are stuck with them (216).

In a sense the Third World has even fewer options in this regard than the West—as the current debt crisis and consequent structural adjustments make clear. Young people in the West have the luxury to drop out of the rat race and travel the world to "find themselves"; their counterparts in the Third World scramble for the coveted places in secondary schools or the scarce job openings. Neither they nor their elders have the time or the resources to propose alternative methods of economic growth.

The most they can hope for is to humanize the process—which indeed is not a small thing. For the peoples of the Third World still are able to foster personal and community values, they are able to maintain spaces in their lives for each other and for God. This spiritual and human sensitivity is the great contribution of their theologies; but their inability to come to terms creatively with the modern world is their corresponding weakness. If their voice of protest is welcome, even essential to us, their continuing powerlessness and poverty must remain intolerable both for us and for them.

It should be clear by now what exchange the theologies in the West and those in the Third World are called to make. We in the West have made ourselves masters of every situation, materially and politically speaking. We have in a very real sense gained the world. But for too many this progress has had a very high price tag: broken relationships and broken health, a harried lifestyle that leaves no time for people or for God, and a growing blindness to the sparkle and brightness of the presence of God in all of life. Our theology reflects and wrestles with this spiritual poverty, called variously secularism or scientism, but it is not clear that progress is being made.

This poverty at the same time is the obverse, some would argue the necessary consequence, of our strength. Western civilization, even the Enlightenment and its secularism, can be shown to rest on the revolutionary changes in consciousness made possible by the Reformation. There the unified civilization of the Middle Ages was broken up and the world was desacralized—as the entire range of art and literature illustrates. This, it can be argued, is the direct fruit of the rediscovery of the freedom of men and women to stand responsible before God in his world (cf. Abraham Kuyper, 1956). This freedom, of course, allows persons to deal with their setting apart from God—what Karl Barth calls the impossible possibility—but it has allowed them to explore, develop, and discover the world. In spite of the growing secularism, then, and in part because of it, theology in the West continues its exploration of the human and human freedom in creation. It has focused on the major problems of modernization: technology, economic development, the environment, peace studies, and the media (including the complexities of translating and interpreting Scripture). These areas are of extreme urgency not only in the West but also in the developing world.

The lack of serious interaction with these issues, I have said, is the weakness of theological reflection in the Third World. Although there are exceptions, Cyril Okorocha's recent thesis is an example. But this weakness too is the reverse of the strength of Third World theologians, for those theologians have insisted on maintaining their values, even at the expense of their own "progress." These very human treasures that they hold to are the very things we hunger and thirst after and our children are scouring the world to find. Perhaps if we are quiet long enough to listen, lines of communication will be opened. When this happens, perhaps our brothers and sisters in the Third World, knowing they have something to say, will again be in a position to hear from us this time not as pupils, but as equals, who have their word of criticism as well as of appreciation.

But if we have heard what our brothers and sisters have been saying in Latin America we cannot leave things here. For the question comes back: Why have we not listened? And why is it that so many in the developing world live in misery, while we have more than we need? Is there some fundamental imbalance that needs to be addressed? If the dependency model that liberation theology has proposed has any validity, Christians from all parts of the world must be concerned with this most important issue of our interrelation. And whatever their political presupposition, they must be willing to ask what relevance the Jubilee Christ announced in Luke 4:18–21 has for this global distortion.

Finally, I must make two warning comments. The first relates to the general weakness of biblical exposition in relation to the issues of each region (with the exception we have noted in Latin America). If our assumption is valid, that only Scripture is finally valid as God's revelation of himself across cultures, this should concern us greatly. For only as we engage in a serious reading of Scripture in terms of our setting will we tap the real power of God's Word. Restoring biblical exposition to its place of centrality may well stimulate theology in all areas: the Third World to see the importance both of God's present and future program of renewing the earth; the West to regain the centrality of human and community values in the context of global righteousness.

The second warning is that all too often both in the West and abroad, the study of Scripture is abstracted from its setting. Or we bring to our reading a theological grid that is alien to Scripture—we have seen the harm that Teilhard de Chardin has done in influencing biblical interpretation both in Latin America and in Asia. Only as we hold our theological frameworks as "working hypotheses," as Father Arevalo put it, will we let Scripture have the final word. We have seen how this is beginning to happen in various parts of the world, and this gives us a hopeful glimpse of our growing up together into Christ (Eph. 4:15).

In conclusion, I return to the point I made at the beginning of this chapter. Theology is meant to serve our witness and discipleship in our particular setting. It plays a critical and ordering function in witness and worship (cf. von Allmen, 1975). While we take these discussions as starting points and these strategies as models, we must not suppose that we are after some grand synthesis—a kind of universal theology that will apply in every place. It is clear by now that we cannot expect this, at least not until we stand before Christ. Even then each perspective will have its special role to play, like so many pieces in a grand mosaic. For theology arises from the missionary encounter between Scripture, the Christ of Scripture, and our particular setting. Thus theology done on earth will surely bear the marks of its setting. But in the end those very marks and the slant they give to our reading will make an authentic contribution to a living theology. For this we work and pray.

SELECTED BIBLIOGRAPHY

A. *General*: On methodology and non-Western traditions in theology

Carlos H. Abesamis
1988 *A Third Look at Jesus*. Quezon City, Philippines: Claretian Publications.

Gerald H. Anderson and Thomas F. Stransky, eds.
1976 *Mission Trends No. 3: Third World Theologies*. New York: Paulist and Grand Rapids: Eerdmans.

Norman Anderson, ed.
1976 *The World's Religions*. Downers Grove: InterVarsity.

David B. Barrett
1988 "Annual Statistical Table on Global Mission." *International Bulletin of Missionary Research*. 12/1:16.

Peter Berger
1976 *Pyramids of Sacrifice*. New York: Doubleday.

Peter Berger, et al.
1973 *The Homeless Mind: Modernization and Consciousness*. New York: Random House.

Stephen Bevans
1985 "Models of Contextual Theology,"*Missiology*. 13/2:185–202.

Herbert Blumer
1969 *Symbolic Interactionism: Perspective and Method*. Berkeley: University of California Press.

Robert McAfee Brown
1984 *Unexpected News: Reading the Bible with Third World Eyes*. Philadelphia: Westminster.

Walbert Buhlmann
1977 *The Coming of the Third Church*. Maryknoll: Orbis.

197

Harvie M. Conn
1984 *Eternal Word and Changing Worlds: Theology, Anthropology, and Mission in Trialogue.* Grand Rapids: Academie Books, Zondervan.

John Driver
1986 *Understanding the Atonement for the Mission of the Church.* Scottdale: Herald.

James D. G. Dunn
1980 *Christology in the Making: An Inquiry into the Origins of the Doctrine of the Incarnation.* London: SCM.

William Dyrness
1983 *Christian Apologetics in a World Community.* Downers Grove: InterVarsity
1989 *How Does America Hear the Gospel?* Grand Rapids: Eerdmans.
1989A "A Unique Opportunity: Christianity in the World Today, A Globe-circling Appraisal." *14th Mission Handbook.* Monrovia, Calif.: MARC (World Vision): 7–20.

H. Byron Earhart
1984 *Religion of Japan.* San Francisco: Harper.

Mircea Eliade
1958 *Patterns in Comparative Religion.* London: Sheed and Ward.

Jean Galot
1981 *The Person of Christ: Covenant Between God and Man.* Rome: Gregorian University.

Clifford Geertz
1983 *Local Knowledge: Further Essays in Interpretive Anthropology.* New York: Basic Books.

Jerry Gill
1971 *The Possibility of Religious Knowledge.* Grand Rapids: Eerdmans.

James P. Grant
1989 *The State of the World's Children.* New York and London: Oxford University Press (for UNICEF).

Paul Harrison
1979 *Inside the Third World.* Middlesex: Penguin.

Paul Hiebert
1982 "The Flaw of the Excluded Middle." *Missiology.* 10/1:35–47.

Paul and Frances F. Hiebert
1987 *Case Studies in Missions.* Grand Rapids: Baker.

SELECTED BIBLIOGRAPHY

David J. Hesselgrave
1968 *Communicating Christ Cross-Culturally.* Grand Rapids: Academie Books, Zondervan.

Charles H. Kraft
1979 *Christianity in Culture.* Maryknoll: Orbis.
1983 *Communication Theory for Christian Witness.* Nashville: Abingdon.

Abraham Kuyper
1956 *Lectures on Calvinism.* Grand Rapids: Eerdmans.

Johannes Metz
1969 *Theology of the World.* New York: Herder.

Stephen Neill
1964 *A History of Christian Missions.* Middlesex: Penguin.
1976 *Jesus Through Many Eyes: Introduction to the Theology of the New Testament.* Philadelphia: Fortress.

Benjamin Nelson
1981 *On the Roads to Modernity: Conscience, Science and Civilization.* Totowa, N.J.: Bowman and Littlefield.

Lesslie Newbigin
1983 *The Other Side of 1984.* Geneva: World Council of Churches.
1986 *Foolishness to the Greeks: The Gospel and Western Culture.* Grand Rapids: Eerdmans.

Bruce J. Nicholls
1979 *Contextualization: A Theology of Gospel and Culture.* Downers Grove: InterVarsity.

Michael Polanyi
1958 *Personal Knowledge: Toward a Post-critical Philosophy.* London: Routledge and Kegan Paul.

Klaas Runia
1984 *The Present-day Christological Debate.* Downers Grove: InterVarsity.

Vinay Samuel and Chris Sugden, eds.
1983 *Sharing Jesus in the "Two Thirds" World.* Grand Rapids: Eerdmans.

Robert J. Schreiter
1985 *Constructing Local Theologies.* Maryknoll: Orbis.

Seoul Declaration
1983 *Evangelical Review of Theology.* 7/1.

Dorothee Soelle
1974 *Political Theology.* Philadelphia: Fortress.

Krister Stendahl
1976 "The Apostle Paul and the Introspective Conscience of the West." In *Paul Among Jews and Gentiles.* Philadelphia: Fortress. Pp. 78–96.

John R. W. Stott
1975 *Christian Mission in the Modern World.* Downers Grove: InterVarsity.

John R. W. Stott and Robert T. Coote
1980 *Down to Earth: Essays on Gospel and Culture.* Grand Rapids: Eerdmans.

Charles Taylor
1985 *Philosophy and the Human Sciences: Philosophical Papers 2.* Cambridge University Press. 1982.

n.a.
n.d. *Teologia Desde el Tercer Munda: Documentos Finales de los cinco Congresos Internacionales de la Asociacion Ecumenica de teologos del Tercer Mundo.* San Jose, Costa Rica: DEI.

Sergio Torres and Virginia Fabella, eds.
1978 *The Emergent Gospel: Theology from the Underside of History.* Maryknoll: Orbis.

David Tracy
1975 *The Blessed Rage for Order.* New York: Seabury.

Johannes Verkuyl
1978 *Contemporary Missiology: An Introduction.* Grand Rapids: Eerdmans.

G. F. Vicedon, ed.
1972 "Christ and the Younger Churches." *Africa Theological Journal.*

Daniel Von Allmen
1975 "The Birth of Theology." *International Review of Missions.* 44 (1975): 37–55.

A. F. Walls
1976 "Towards an Understanding of Africa's Place in Christian History." In *Religion in a Pluralistic Society.* J. S. Pobee, ed. Leiden: Brill. Pp. 180–89.

B. *African Theology*

Chinua Achebe
1958 *Things Fall Apart.* London: Heinemann.
1987 *Anthills of the Savannah.* Nairobi: Heinemann Kenya.

SELECTED BIBLIOGRAPHY

Tokunboh Adeyemo
1979 *Salvation in African Tradition.* Nairobi: Evangel Publishing House.
1983 "Toward an Evangelical African Theology," *Evangelical Review of Theology.* 7/l:147–54.

Kofi Appiah-Kubi and Sergio Torres, eds.
1979 *African Theology en Route.* Maryknoll: Orbis.

David B. Barrett
1968 *Schism and Renewal in Africa.* London: Oxford University Press.

Kwame Bediako
1983 "Identity and Integration: An Inquiry into the Nature and Problems of Indigenization in Selected Early Hellenistic and Modern African Christian Writers." Ph.D. Thesis. University of Aberdeen.
1983A "Biblical Christologies in the Context of African Traditional Religions." In Samuel and Sugden, eds. 1983:81–121.
1989 "The Roots of African Theology." *International Bulletin.* 13/2:58–65.

Jon Bonk
1980 "All Things to All Persons: The Missionary as a Racist-Imperialist." *Missiology.* 8/3:285–306.

F. Eboussi Boulaga
1984 *Christianity Without Fetishes: An African Critique and Recapture of Christianity.* Maryknoll: Orbis.

Kwesi A. Dickson
1984 *Theology in Africa.* London: Darton, Longman and Todd.

Kwesi A. Dickson and Paul Ellingworth, eds.
1971 *Biblical Revelation and African Belief.* Maryknoll: Orbis.

A. Ekwunife
1987 "African Culture: A Definition." *African Christian Studies.* 3/3:5–18.

E. E. Evans-Pritchard
1956 *Nuer Religion.* Oxford University Press.

Edward W. Fashole-Luke
1976 "The Quest for African Christian Theologies." *Scottish Journal of Theology.* 29:159–175.
1981 "Footpaths and Signposts to African Christian Theologies." *Scottish Journal of Theology.* 34:385–414.

John C. Ganly
1985 "Evil Spirits in Pastoral Practice." *Afar.* 26/6:345–50.

Richard J. Gehman
1987 *Doing African Christian Theology: An Evangelical Perspective.* Nairobi: Evangel.

Dean S. Gilliland
1986 "How 'Christian' are African Independent Churches?" *Missiology.* xiv/3:259–72.

David M. Gitari and G. Patrick Benson, eds.
1986 *Witnessing to the Living God in Contemporary Africa.* Nairobi: Africa Theological Fraternity.

J. Gatunga Githiga
1984 *The Spirit in the Black Soul.* Nairobi: Evangel.

Mark E. Glasswell and Edward W. Fashole-Luke
1974 *New Testament Christianity for Africa and the World: Essays in Honour of Harry Sawyerr.* London: SPCK.

E. Bolaji Idowu
1965 *Towards an Indigenous Church.* Oxford University Press. Reprinted by Methodist Church in Nigeria, 1973.
1973 *African Traditional Religion: A Definition.* London: SCM.

Osadolor Imasogie
1983 *Guidelines for Christian Theology in Africa.* Accra: Africa Christian Press.

Bennetta Jules-Rosette
1975 *African Apostles: Ritual and Conversion in the Church of John Maranke.* Ithaca: Cornell University Press.

Byang H. Kato
1975 *Theological Pitfalls in Africa.* Kisumu, Kenya: Evangel.

Noel Q. King
1986 *African Cosmos: An Introduction to Religion in Africa.* Belmont, Calif.: Wadsworth.

Michael C. Kirwen
1987 *The Missionary and the Diviner: Contending Theologies of Christian and African Religions.* Maryknoll: Orbis.

Ali A. Mazrui
1980 *The African Condition.* London: Heinemann.

John S. Mbiti
1969 *Africans Religions and Philosophy.* London: Heinemann.
1971 *New Testament Eschatology in an African Background.* Oxford University Press.
1975 *The Prayers of African Religion.* Maryknoll: Orbis.
1986 *Bible and Theology in African Christianity.* Nairobi: Oxford University Press.

SELECTED BIBLIOGRAPHY

Emefie Ikenga Metuh
1981 *God and Man in African Religion*. London: Geoffrey Chapman.

Gwinyai H. Muzorewa
1985 *The Origins and Development of African Theology*. Maryknoll: Orbis.

Ngugi Wa Thiong'o
1965 *The River Between*. London: Heinemann.

Charles Nyamiti
n.d. African Tradition and the Christian God. Eldoret, Kenya: Gaba.
1984 *Christ our Ancestor: Christology from an African Perspective*. Gweru, Zimbabwe: Mambo Press.

Mercy Amba Oduyoye
1986 *Hearing and Knowing: Theological Reflections on Christianity in Africa*. Maryknoll: Orbis.

Cyril Okorocha
1987 *The Meaning of Religious Conversion in Africa: The Case of the Igbo of Nigeria*. Aldershot, Hampshire: Avebury-Gower.

Nlenanya Onwu
1986 "Debate on African Theology Revisited." *Revue Africaine de Thelogie*. 10/19:31–41.

John Parratt, ed.
1987 *A Reader in African Theology*. London: SPCK.

E. G. Parrinder
1974 *African Traditional Religion*. London: Sheldon (3rd ed.)

Okot P'Bitek
1970 *African Religions in Western Scholarship*. Kampala: East African Literature Bureau.

John S. Pobee
1979 *Toward an African Theology*. Nashville: Abingdon.

John S. Pobee, ed.
1976 *Religion in a Pluralistic Society*. Leiden: Brill.

Eugene Rubingh
1974 "The African Shape of the Gospel." *Impact* (USA), (March 1974):3–5.

Harry Sawyerr
1968 *Creative Evangelism: Towards a New Christian Encounter with Africa*. London: Lutterworth.

Aylward Shorter
1974 *African Culture and the Christian Church: An Introduction to Social and Pastoral Anthropology*. Maryknoll: Orbis.

1977 *African Christian Theology: Adaptation or Incarnation.* Maryknoll: Orbis.

John V. Taylor
1963 *The Primal Vision: Christian Presence amid African Religion.* London: SCM.

Placide Tempels
1949 *Bantu Philosophy* (ET Colin King). Paris: Presence Africaine.

Tite Tienou
1983 "Biblical Foundations: An African Study." *Evangelical Review of Theology.* 7/1:89–101.

Lester van Essen
1977 "The African Independent Church." *Reformed Journal.* (October 1977):14–17.

Kwasi Wiredu
1980 *Philosophy and an African Culture.* Cambridge University Press.

Richard A. Wright, ed.
1979 *African Philosophy.* Washington: University Press of America, (2nd ed.).

Evan M. Zuesse
1985 *Ritual Cosmos: The Sanctification of Life in African Religions.* Athens, Ohio: Ohio University Press.

C. *Latin American Theology*

Rubem A. Alves
1969 *A Theology of Human Hope.* Washington: Corpus.

Mortimer Arias
1980 "Hope and Despair in Latin America." *Occasional Essays* (San Jose). XIII/1,2 (June): 19–43.

Clodovis Boff
1987 *Theology and Praxis: Epistemological Foundations.* Maryknoll: Orbis.

Leonardo Boff
1978 *Jesus Christ Liberator: A Critical Christology for our Time.* Maryknoll: Orbis.
1986 *Ecclesiogenesis.* Maryknoll: Orbis.

Leonardo Boff and C. Boff
1987 *Introducing Liberation Theology.* Maryknoll: Orbis.

Jose Miguez Bonino
1971 "New Theological Perspective." *Religious Education.* 66(6):403–11.

1975 Doing Theology in a Revolutionary Situation. Philadelphia: Fortress.
1976 Christians and Marxists: The Mutual Challenge to Revolution. Grand Rapids: Eerdmans.
1983 Toward a Christian Political Ethic. Philadelphia: Fortress Press.

Eduardo Bonnin
1982 Espiritualidad y Liberacíon en América Latina. San Jose: DEI.

Mark Lau Branson and C. René Padilla, eds.
1986 Conflict and Context: Hermeneutics in the Americas. Grand Rapids: Eerdmans.

Robert McAfee Brown
1978 Theology in a New Key: Responding to Liberation Themes. Philadelphia: Westminster.

Guillermo Cook
1987 "Grassroots Churches and Reformation in Central America." Latin American Pastoral Issues (San Jose). XIV/1:5–23.

Orlando E. Costas
1982 Christ Outside the Gate: Mission Beyond Christendom. Maryknoll: Orbis.

Alejandro Cussianovich
1979 Religious Life and the Poor: Liberation Theology Perspectives. Maryknoll: Orbis.

Carolina Maria de Jesus
1962 Child of the Dark: Diary of Carolina Maria de Jesus. New York: Mentor (New American Library).

Enrique Düssel
1974 The History of the Church in Latin America: An Interpretation. San Antonio, Texas: Mexican-American Cultural Center.
1976 History and the Theology of Liberation. Maryknoll: Orbis.
1981 A History of the Church in Latin America (ET Alan Neely). Grand Rapids: Eerdmans.

Douglas J. Elwood
1987 "Social Analysis, Theological Reflection and Pastoral Planning." Asia Journal of Theology. 1/1:130–44.

Samuel Escobar
1987 La Fe Evangelica y las Teologias de la Liberacion. El Paso, Texas: Casa Bautista.
1987A "Base Church Communities: A Historical Perspective." Latin American Pastoral Issues. XIV/1:24–33.

Samuel Escobar, Pedro Arana, Valdir Steurnagel, and Rodrigo Zapata
1983 "A Latin America Critique of Latin American Theology."
 Evangelical Review of Theology. 7/1:48–62.

Francis P. Fiorenza
1974 "Latin American Liberation Theology." *Interpretation*. 28:441–57.

Austin Flannery, ed.
1975 *Vatican Council II: The Conciliar and Post-conciliar Documents*. Northport, N.Y.: Costello.

Paulo Freire
1972 *Pedagogy of the Oppressed*. Harmondsworth, Middlesex: Penguin.

Denis Goulet
1974 *A New Moral Order: Development Ethics and Liberation Theology*. Maryknoll: Orbis.

Brian Griffiths
1982 *Morality and the Market Place*. London: Hodder and Stoughton.

Christine E. Gudorf
1987 "Liberation Theology's Use of Scripture: A Response to First World Critics." *Interpretation*. (January): 5–18.

Gustavo Gutiérrez
1973 *A Theology of Liberation*. Maryknoll: Orbis.
1984 *We Drink From Our Own Wells*. Maryknoll: Orbis.

Thomas D. Hanks
1983 *God So Loved the Third World: The Bible, the Reformation and Liberation Theologies*. Maryknoll: Orbis.

R. Allen Hatch
1985 "The Challenge of Liberation Theology." *Occasional Essays*. XII/1:5–15.

Joe Holland and Peter Henriot
1983 *Social Analysis*. Washington: Center of Concern (2nd ed).

Raymond C. Hundley
1987 *Radical Liberation Theology: An Evangelical Response*. Wilmore, Ky.: Bristol.

Alistair Kee, ed.
1974 *A Reader in Political Theology*. London: SCM.

J. Andrew Kirk
1979 *Liberation Theology: An Evangelical View from the Third World*. Atlanta: John Knox.
1980 *Theology Encounters Revolution*. Downers Grove: InterVarsity.

J. B. Libanio
1987 "Base Church Communities in Socio-Cultural Perspective" *Latin America Pastoral Issues* (San Jose). XIV/1:34–47.

Juan A Mackay
1957 *Prefacio a la Teleogía Cristiana.* Mexico City: Cambridge University Press (2nd ed.).

Pedrito U. Maynard-Reid
1987 *Poverty and Wealth in James.* Maryknoll: Orbis.

Dennis P. McCann
1981 *Christian Realism and Liberation Theology: Practical Theologies in Creative Conflict.* Maryknoll: Orbis.

José Miranda
1974 *Marx and the Bible: A Critique of the Philosophy of Oppression.* Maryknoll: Orbis.

Jürgen Moltmann
1976 "An Open Letter to José Miguez Bonino." *Christianity and Crisis.* (March 29): 57–63.

Emilio Nuñez
1985 *Liberation Theology.* Chicago: Moody Press.

C. René Padilla
1972 "Theology in Latin America." *Theological News Monographs.* #5.
1980 "Hermeneutics and Culture: A Theological Persective." In Stott and Coote. *Down to Earth.* Eerdmans.
1983 "Biblical Foundations: A Latin American Study." *Evangelical Review of Theology.* 7/1:79–88.
1985 *Mission Between the Times: Essays on the Kingdom.* Grand Rapids: Eerdmans.

Joseph Ratzinger
1984 *Instruction on Certain Aspects of Theology of Liberation.* Rome: Sacred Congregation for the Doctrine of the Faith.

Pablo Richard
1985 *The Church Born by the Force of God in Central America.* New York: Circus.

Pablo Richard, ed.
1981 *Materiales para una historia de la teología en America Latina.* San Jose, Costa Rica: Departamento Ecumenico de Investigaciones (DEI).
1985 *Raices de la teología latinoamericana.* San Jose: DEI.

Sidney Rooy
1986 "Social Revolution and the Future of the Church." *Occasional Essays.* XIII/1,2 (June): 60–89.

Julio de Santa Ana
1978 *Separation Without Hope: The Church and the Poor During the Industrial Revolution and Colonial Expansion.* Maryknoll: Orbis.

Juan Luis Segundo
1974 *Our Idea of God.* Maryknoll: Orbis.
1976 *The Liberation of Theology.* Maryknoll: Orbis.
1983 "The Shift within Latin American Theology." Lecture given at Regis College, Toronto, 22 March 1983.

Richard Shaull
1984 *Heralds of a New Reformation: The Poor in South and North America.* Maryknoll: Orbis.

Jon Sobrino
1978 *Christology at the Crossroads.* Maryknoll: Orbis.
1987 *Jesus in Latin America.* Maryknoll: Orbis.

Elsa Tamez
1982 *Bible of the Oppressed.* Maryknoll: Orbis.

Sergio Torres and John Eagleson
1976 *Theology in the Americas.* Maryknoll: Orbis.

Miroslav Volf
1983 "Doing and Interpreting: An Examination of the Relationship Between Theory and Practice in Latin American Liberation Theology." *Themelios*, April: 11–19.

D. *Asian Theology*

Daniel J. Adams
1987 *Cross Cultural Theology: Western Reflections in Asia.* Atlanta: John Knox.

A. J. Appasamy
1958 *Sundar Singh: A Biography.* London: Lutterworth.

Robert D. Baird and Alfred Bloom
1971 *Indian and Far Eastern Religious Traditions.* New York: Harper & Row.

J. R. Chandran
1978 "Development of Christian Theology in India: A Critical Survey." In Torres and Fabella, ed. *The Emergent Gospel.* Maryknoll: Orbis.

Samuel H. Chao
1987 "Confucian Chinese and the Gospel: Methodological Considerations." *Asian Journal of Theology.* 1/1: 17–36.

SELECTED BIBLIOGRAPHY

Saral K. Chatterji
1980 "Some Ingredients of a Theology of the People." *Religion and Society.* xxvii/4: 3–28.

Khin Maung Din
1975 "Some Problems and Possibilities for Burmese Christian Theology Today." *Southeast Asia Journal of Theology.* 16/2:17–30.

Richard H. Drummond
1971 *A History of Christianity in Japan.* Grand Rapids: Eerdmans.

W. A. Dyrness
1979 *Christian Art in Asia.* Amsterdam: Rodopi.

Douglas J. Elwood
1975 "Christian Theology in an Asian Setting: The Gospel and Chinese Intellectual Culture." *Southeast Asia Journal of Theology.* 16/2:1–16.

Douglas J. Elwood, ed.
1976 *What Asian Christians Are Thinking.* Quezon City: New Day (Later published as *Asian Christian Theology: Emerging Themes.* Philadelphia: Westminster.)

Shusaku Endo
1969 *Silence.* (ET William Johnston). Tokyo: Sophia University Press.

John C. England, ed.
1982 *Living Theology in Asia.* Maryknoll: Orbis.

Virginia Fabella, ed.
1980 *Asia's Struggle for Full Humanity.* Maryknoll: Orbis.

Yu-Lan Fung
1962 *The Spirit of Chinese Philosophy.* Boston: Beacon.

Zhao Fusan
1986 *Christianity in China.* Manila: De La Salle University Press.

Han Chul-Ha
1983 "An Asian Criticism of Western Theology." *Evangelical Review of Theology.* 7/1: 34–47.

Earl Stanley Jones
1925 *The Christ of the Indian Road.* Nashville: Abingdon.

Kazoh Kitamori
1965 *A Theology of the Pain of God.* Richmond: John Knox.

Kosuke Koyama
1974 *Waterbuffalo Theology.* Maryknoll: Orbis.
1976 *No Handle on the Cross.* London: SCM.

Wing-Hung Lam
1983 *Chinese Theology in Construction.* Pasadena: William Carey Library.

Antonio B. Lambino, Edmundo M. Martinez, Carlos H. Abesamis, and C. G. Arevalo
1977 *Towards "Doing Theology" in the Philippine Context: Four Papers.* Manila: *Loyola Papers,* no. 9.

Jung Young Lee
1974 *God Suffers for Us: A Systematic Inquiry into a Concept of Divine Passibility.* The Hague: Martinus Nijhoff.

David Lim
1986 "A Plea for an 'Ethics of the Cross.' " *Transformation.* 3/4: 1–5.

Frank Lynch, ed.
1964 *Four Readings on Philippine Culture.* Quezon City: Ateneo de Manila. *IPC Papers,* no. 2.

Jürgen Moltmann
1981 *The Trinity and the Kingdom.* San Francisco: Harper & Row.

Gyoji Nabetani
1983 "An Asian Critique of Church Movements in Japan." *Evangelical Review of Theology.* 7/1: 73–78.

Emerito P. Nacpil and Douglas J. Elwood, eds.
1978 *The Human and the Holy: Asian Perspectives in Christian Theology.* Quezon City: New Day (US edition: 1980, Maryknoll: Orbis).

Stephen Neill
1976 *Salvation Tomorrow.* London: Lutterworth.

G. C. Oosthuizen
1972 *Theological Battleground in Asia and Africa: The Issues Facing the Churches and the Efforts to Overcome Western Divisions.* London: C. Hurst.

Geoffrey Parrinder
1982 *Avatar and Incarnation: A Comparison of Indian and Christian Beliefs.* New York: Oxford University Press.

William Pfaff
1989 "For China the March Drags on." *International Herald Tribune.* (May 12), 6.

Aloysius Pieris
1979 "Towards an Asian Theology of Liberation: Some Religio-Cultural Guidelines." *Dialogue* (Colombo), vii: 29-50. (Reprinted frequently. cf. Pieris, 1988, and Fabella, ed., 1980)
1988 *An Asian Theology of Liberation.* Maryknoll: Orbis.

SELECTED BIBLIOGRAPHY

Samuel Rayan
1976 "Indian Theology and the Problem of History" in *Society and Religion: Essays in Honor of M. M. Thomas.* Richard Taylor, ed. Madras: Christian Literature Society.

Bong Rin Ro and Ruth Eshenaur, eds.
1984 *The Bible and Theology in Asian Contexts: An Evangelical Perspective.* Taichung, Taiwan: Asia Theological Association.

S. J. Samartha
1974 *Hindu Response to the Unbound Christ.* Madras: Christian Literature Society.

Vinay Samuel and Chris Sugden, eds.
1983 *Sharing Jesus in the Two Thirds World.* Grand Rapids: Eerdmans.

C. S. Song
1975 *Christian Mission in Reconstruction: An Asian Analysis.* Maryknoll: Orbis.
1984 *Tell Us Our Names: Story Theology from an Asian Perspective.* Maryknoll: Orbis.
1986 *Theology From the Womb of Asia.* Maryknoll: Orbis.

Sunand Sumithra and Bruce Nicholls
1983 "Towards an Evangelical Theology in India." *Evangelical Review of Theology.* 7/1: 172–82.

S. Takayanago
1979 "Between Fact and Truth—Endo Shusaku's Powerless Jesus." *Japan Missionary Bulletin* 33:608–14.

Masao Takenaka
1986 *God is Rice: Asian Culture and Christian Faith.* Geneva: World Council of Churches.

Rodrigo D. Tano
1983 "Towards an Evangelical Asian Theology." *Evangelical Review of Theology.* 7/1: 155–71.

M. M. Thomas
1969 *The Acknowledged Christ of the Indian Renaissance.* London: SCM.

INDEX

Ablutions, 41
Achebe, C., 35, 40
Advaitin, 131, 177
Africa, 12–17, 23, 33, 35–70, 124
  South, 35–36
The *African Condition* (A. Mazrui), 69
African Inland Church, 62
African Independent Churches, 41, 62
African Traditional Religions, 39, 68, 168
Africanization, 36
Agape, 125
AIDS, 23
Akamba tribe (Africa), 48, 59–60, 62
Akan tribe (Africa), 168
Alliance for Progress, 77–78, 81
Alves, R., 73, 79
America, North, 13, 83
Analects, 136
Analysis of culture. See Culture.
Anarchy, 124
Ancestors (in African religion), 47
  and Christ, 166–70
The *Acknowledged Christ of the Indian Renaissance* (M. M. Thomas), 129
Anicca (impermanence), 133
Animism, 124
Anitta (soullessness), 133
Anointing, 41
Anthropology, 21–22, 25
Appasamy, A. J., 127, 130
Arcio, S., 82

Arevalo, C. G., 153, 154, 195
Arias, M., 81
Arms race, 23
Art, 15
Ashanti tribe (Africa), 48, 59–60
Asia, 13–17, 25, 32
Asian theology. See Theology.
Asian Theological Conference (Sri Lanka, 1979), 151
Atheist, 103
Atman, 122
Atonement, theories of, 172
Augustine, 67, 182

Bakaonde tribe (Africa), 56
Bakhti tradition, 127, 130
Bandung Conference, 12–13
Base Communities, 41, 82, 99, 101, 104
Barreiro, J., 76
Barrett, D., 37, 41
Bediako, K. (Ghana), 40, 47, 50, 57–58, 60, 66, 168–70
Bengali literature, 126
Bennett, J. C., 83
Berbers (N. Africa), 67
Berger, P., 192–93
Berlin Conference, 38
Bevans, S., 25
Bhagavad Gita, 122, 123, 127
Bible, biblical, 27, 40, 90, 129
  circles, 99, 102
  exposition, weakness of in Third World, 195
  See *also* Scripture.
Blood sacrifices. See Sacrifices.
Blumer, H., 22

Boff, C., 80, 114, 115
Boff, L., 81–82, 100–102, 171
Boff, C. and L., 97
Bonk, Jon, 38
Bonnin, E., 103, 106
"Born Again," 28
Bourgeois, 80
Brahman, 122, 123
Brahmins, 125
Buddha, 123, 133, 138, 147
Buddhism, 121, 123, 124, 132–34, 144, 161
Buhlmann, W., 189–90
Bultmann, R., 86, 88
Buthelezei, M., 69

Calvin, J., 92, 103
Camara, H., 81, 92–93
Capitalism, 14, 39, 82, 124, 125, 139
Carey W., 85, 126
Castes, 123, 127, 129–31
Catholic Church, Catholicism, 73–74, 76, 79, 82, 99–100
CEBs (Base Communities in Latin America), 99, 100, 102
CEPAL (Latin America Study Center in Chile), 78
Celebration (in African religions), 63, 97
Chan, W-T., 136
Chandran, J. R., 126, 128
Chi, 49
Chile, 99
Chinese culture, 15, 122, 135–41
   intelligentsia, 135
Chinese theology. See Theology.
Christ, 90–91, 98–100, 103–4, 122, 125, 127–32, 146, 147
   Cosmic reign of, 165, 181
Christ of the Indian Road (E. S. Jones), 128
Christendom, 75, 77–78
Christianity, 35, 38–40, 125, 126, 128, 157
   Ethiopian, 67

European, 66–67, 72, 75
Christology, 63, 97, 134, 154
   African, 166–70
   cross-cultural, 163–84
   functional, 180
   Latin American, 170–75
   trinitarian context of, 182
   unity and diversity in, 163–66
Church, 99–103
   universal, 31
Clan, 40
Cook, G., 99
Cold War, 12
Colonialism, 37, 39, 122, 124
   neo-colonialism, 37, 77, 84, 151
Commerce and missions. See Missions.
Common project, 104
Community, 23–33
   eschatological, 101
Communism, 124. See also Marxism.
Concepts, theological. See Theology.
Cone, J. 88
Confucianism, 136, 138, 139
Conquistadores, 76
Constantinian political framework, 118
Contemplation, 105
Contexts, social, 86
Contextualization, 24, 29, 97
Copernican Revolution, 94
Costas, O., 72, 79, 83, 85, 97
Covenant, 90
cummings, e.e., 185
Crisis of faith in the West, 191
Cross, 172
Cross-cultural knowledge, 21, 23
   casebook (Bible as), 27
   theology, 20, 59
   theory, 21
Culture, 29–31, 34
   analysis of, 29–30

Christianization of, 169
desacralization of, 169
sciences and, 94
social analysis of, 82, 94–94, 98–99, 106
Cyprian, 67

Dar es Salaam, 14
de Chardin, T., 80, 110
de Jesus, Maria Carolina, 967
de Las Casas, B., 76
de Silva, L., 122, 133
Delegates of the Word, 99
Democracy, 124
Desallorismo, 78
Developmentalism, 92
Devil, 39
Diakonia (Greek), 101
Dickson, K., 38, 167
Dinka tribe (Africa), 51
Discipleship, 91, 104
and Christology, 173–75
Divine Lord, 174
Dodd, C. H., 61
Doing African Christian Theology (R. Gehman), 64
Donatists (N. Africa), 67
Driver, J., 164–65
Dukkha (suffering), 133
Dussell, E., 75–77
Dynamic equivalency, 27

Ecclesiogenesis (L. Boff), 100
Economy, economics, 77, 93, 98, 124
dependency of, 78, 80, 84; model of, 112, 195
development of, 77–78
domination of, 72
socio-economic, 26
Ecumenical, 99
Ekwenuike, A., 42
Eliade, M., 140
Elwood, D., 131, 132
End of History, 190
Endo, Shusako (*Silence*), 144

England, 38, 128, 129
Enlightenment, 95, 190–91
Environment, 20, 23
Epistemological privilege, 98
Epistemology of obedience, 115, 116
Epulu tribe (Africa), 49
Eschaton, 129
Escobar, S., 19, 73, 75, 82–84, 91, 94, 99–100, 118, 120
Ethics, medical, 19
Ethnocentrism, 20–21, 38
Eucharist, 100
Europe, European, 13, 38–39
ethnocentrism, 40
intellectualist tradition of, 114
Evangelical, 17–19, 31, 62, 73–74, 83, 102, 127, 130, 131
Fraternity of Evangelical Theologians, 36
See also Seoul Declaration.
Evangelism, 27, 37
Evans-Pritchard, E., 53, 86, 88
Excluded middle, flaw of, 187
Exorcism, 41
Ezeanya, S. N., 47
Ezi-ndu (Igbo: the viable life), 52, 65

Fabella, V., 133, 151
Fabianism, 84
Faith, 95
Family, 16
Fang tribe (Africa), 45
Fashole-Luke, E., 68
Fatalism, 32
Feminism, 20
Filipino values, 151
"First act," 105–6
Forms, cultural and religious, 16, 27, 28
Fragmentation of life, 36
Freedom, 90
Freire, P., 89–90, 130
Fusan, Z., 135
Future, 84–85

Galot, J., 184
Gandy, J., 56
Gaudiem et Spes, 80
Gehman, R., 60, 64
Genesis, book of, 54
Geertz, C., 21–22
Gill, J., 117
Gitari, D., 36
Gnosis, 125
Gospel, 16, 18, 25–29, 31, 33, 35,
    64, 66, 74, 97, 99, 100, 105,
    125, 126, 128, 130, 131, 132,
    134, 135, 140, 144, 147 156,
    159, 162
    and Western culture, 191
    See also Social Gospel.
Goulet, D., 77
Greeks, 75, 89, 91, 130
Griffiths, B., 84
Gudorf, C., 83–84, 106
Gutiérrez, G., 79–82, 97, 105–6,
    120

Han Chul-ha, 161
Hanks, T., 96
Harrison, P., 14
Heathenism, 39, 88
Heritage (in Africa), 40
Hermeneutical circle, 31, 86, 87
Hermeneutical spiral, 31
Hiebert and Hiebert, P. and F., 24
Hiebert, P., 187–88
Hierarchy, 100–101
Hindu, Hinduism, 28, 31, 121–
    27, 131, 132, 140, 142, 157
*The Hindu Response to the Un-
    bound Christ* (S. J. Samar-
    tha), 176–80
Hindu scriptures, 125
Hiroshima, 138
History, historical, 32, 90, 93,
    100, 103, 129, 130
    and Christology, 171, 174, 182
    and God, 107–11
    Latin American, 84
    mediation, 92

"one God-filled," 107
Historiography, 84–85
Holland and Henriot, J. and P.,
    94–95
Holy Spirit, 32, 65, 91
    response to Christ, 176
Hong Kong, 139
Human mediators (in African re-
    ligion), 48–49
Human rights, 82
Humanism, 136

Inca (Latin America), 15
Ideas, 89
Identity, 40, 66
Ideology, ideologies, ideological
    suspicion, 35, 36, 78, 93,
    95–96
    countermodernizing, 192–93
Idowu, B., 31, 39, 42, 46, 63–64,
    68
Igbo tribe (Africa), 43, 45, 49, 52,
    54, 56, 65
Imagination, 41
Imasogie, O., 65
Immanentistic, 95
Imperialism, 38, 84, 135
Incarnation, 153
India, Indians, 24, 28, 33, 122,
    125, 135
Indigenous, 41
Indonesia, 126
Infrastructure, 15
"Inreligionization," 157
*Instruction on Liberation Theol-
    ogy* (J. Ratzinger), 95, 102
Interconnectedness of individ-
    uals and communities, 22
Interest, vested, 93
Interpretive views, 21–22
Islam, 67, 121, 127
Israel, 90

Jaba tribe (Africa), 64
Japan, Japanese, 126, 141–50
Justice, 72, 74, 90

Jesus, 89–90
  humanity of, 173–74, 178
Jubilee, 98, 105
Jesuits, 100
Job, 161
John the Apostle, 120
John XXIII, Pope, 79
Jones, E. S., 128

Kalu, O., 44, 50
Karma, 122, 123, 129, 132, 133
Kato, B., 62, 64
Khin Muang Din, 176, 179
Kikamba language, 60
King, N., 46
Kingdom, 17, 38, 66, 91
  of God, 134, 171
Kirk, A., 89, 93, 112, 116
Kitamori, K., 143
Kitongi, R. B., 49
Koyama, K,. 146–49
Knowledge, sociology of, 86
  autonomous, 86
Kraft, C., 27–29
Kudadjie, J. N., 50–51
Kuyper, A., 194

Lam, W. H., 135
Lambino, A., 153
Language, 21–22
Latin America, Latin Americans,
  12–17, 23 33 41, 70–120,
  124
Lausanne Committee, 14
Lay Christianity, 189
Lee, J. Y., 140 141
Lenin, 84
Lim, D., 123
Libanio, J. B., 100
Liberal, 135
Liberation Theology, 35, 83–84,
  86–99, 102, 104
  Black, 35
  Christology of, 170–75
  Latin American, 69
Livingston, D., 38

Lord, 164
Love, 130
Loyola House of Studies (Ma-
  nila), 153
Lumen Gentium, 99, 101
Luther, Martin, 24

Magic (in African religion), 51
Material dimension of life, 35–
  36
Materialism, 125
Marx, K., 98
Marxism, 15, 78–79, 82–83, 91–
  96, 125, 136, 139
  marxist praxis, *See* Commu-
  nism; Praxis.
Maya, 123
Maya (Latin America), 15
Maynard-Reid, P., 96
Mazrui, A., 15, 69
Mbiti, J., 35–37, 41, 44–45, 47–
  53, 55, 59–64, 68
Mbuti tribe (Africa), 43
Medellin Conference, 80
Memory, 15
Metuh, E., 46, 53–54
Meta-cosmic religions, 124, 157
Miguez Bonino, J., 73, 76–77, 79,
  84, 87, 89–94, 107
Mill, J. S., 117
Miranda, J., 90
Mituki (present, in Kikamba), 61
Missions, 30, 32 37, 39, 56, 66,
  73–74, 76, 122, 135
  commerce and, 38
  missionary strategy of Paul,
  189
  post-missionary Christianity,
  39–40
Modern period, 124
Modernization, 16, 20, 68, 135,
  139, 151, 153, 192–94
  anti-modernist, 135
Moffat, R., 37
Moksha, 123
Moltmann, J., 83, 182

Mystical, mysticism, 74
Muzorewa, G., 36, 47, 57

Nacpil, E., 151, 152
National security, 81
Naturalistic reading of Scripture, 93
Narareth, Jesus of, 132
Nazi, 87
Needs and aspirations, 29
Neill, S., 37, 126, 164
Nelson, B., 22, 186
Newbigin, L., 190–91
New Testament, 89, 101
Ngugi Wa Thiong'o, 40, 83
Nicaragua, 82, 99
Nicholls, B., 130
Nigeria, 14, 39
Nile basin Christianity (Ethio-pian), 67
Nirvana, 122, 123
No Handle on the Cross (K. Koya-ma), 147–48
Noble truths (Buddhism), 123
North African Christianity, 67
Nuer tribal religion (Africa), 53, 55
Nyamiti, C., 45, 58–59, 166–69

Obedience and praxis. See Praxis.
Objective observer, 22
Oduyoye, M., 67
Ohki, H., 158
Okorocha, C., 44–49, 51–52, 56, 58, 62, 64–65, 166, 194
Old Testament, 89, 128
Oligarchies, 93
Omenala (decorum in African religion), 43
Onwu, N., 9, 40
Oxford, 127

Pacific Islands, 126
Padilla, R., 74, 83, 90–91, 96, 106, 119, 174–75

Pagan, 39
Panikkar, K. M., 124
Parallel themes (from Scripture and culture), 31
Parrinder, E. G., 39, 42, 48
Pastoral circle, 96
Paul, 130
Pentecostal Church (in Latin America), 83
People of God, 106
Pfaff, W., 124
Philippians, letter to, 12, 95
Philippines, 121, 126, 150–53
Philosophy, 22–23, 61, 89, 94, 121, 123, 125
  Greek, 86
Pierce, C., 117
Pieris, A., 124, 134, 135, 151, 155, 157
Pluralism, 95
Polanyi, M., 117
pneuma (spirit, Greek), 133
Politics, political process, 23, 41, 93, 99
  liberation, 26
  place of interpreter, 111
Poor, poverty, 72, 74–75, 80–81, 96–99, 121, 134, 187
Power, 23, 26–27, 33, 72, 101
  in African theology, 169
  in Christology, 180
Praxis, practice, 86, 89–91, 94, 112, 115
  model, 26
  Marxist, 95
  obedience and, 112, 113
  ortho, 88
  theory and, 116
Prayer, 27, 40
Presuppositions, 29
Pre-theoretical commitment (to liberation), 116
Prophet, 89
Protestants, 142
  in Latin America, 73–83

Pueblo Conference, 96, 100

Rahner, K., 110
Rationalism, 95
    Cartesian, 161
Ratzinger, J., 95, 98, 102
Rauschenbush, W., 83
Rayan, S., 129–30, 159
Reality, social, 80, 131
Reciprocal worship (Africa), 58
Redemption, 89
Reductionism, 85, 93, 98, 130
Reformation, Protestant, 102, 194
Relativism, 21
Religious ceremony, 33
Renewal movement, 100
    and third world theology, 188
Re-reading (of Scripture), 94
Restructuring (of society), 92
Resurrection, 129, 151
    communal, 167
    historical, 172
Revelation, 21–22, 41
Revolution, revolutionary, 83,
    87, 93
Ricci, M., 125
Richard, P., 84, 102–4
Ritual, 21, 41
The River Between (Ngugi Wa
    Thiong'o), 40
Romans, letter to, 54–55
Roots, 40
Rooy, S., 87
Roy, R. M., 126
Runia, K., 183

Sacrament, sacramental, 101–3
Sacred, 35
Sacrifices, 33–34
    in African religion, 51, 53
Salvation, 90, 111, 124, 130, 142
Samartha, S. J., 131, 132, 149,
    176–80
Samuel and Sugden, V. and C.,
    85, 130, 131, 156, 178–79
Sankara, 123, 131

Sawyerr, H., 41, 49, 51, 59
Scripture, 16, 19, 20, 22–24, 26,
    28–34, 65, 88–90, 97, 99
    102, 133
    in Christology, 182–83
    functionalism of, 91
    in theology, 195
    transcultural, 17, 27, 31
Secular, secularism, 20, 35, 143
Segundo, J., 78, 81–82, 86, 88,
    93, 95, 104, 108, 109
Self, 122, 133
Self-definition, 22
Sen, K. C., 126
Seoul Declaration, 35, 71, 155
Shintoism, 142
Shona tribe (Africa), 47
Sikh, 126
Sin, 53–55, 94, 99
Singh, Sundar, 126–28
Slavery, 38
Sobrino, J., 170–73
Social Gospel, 83
Social science, 20–21, 92, 94
    in theology, 111–12
Sociology, 22
    of knowledge, 86
    Marxist, 95
Sociological analysis, 91
Soelle, D., 23
Sofola, Z., 60
Son of Man, 164
Song, C. S., 137–41, 178
Soteriology, 125, 157
Southeast Asia, 150–55
Spirit of Jesus, 172
Spirits (in African religion), 46–
    47
Spiritual, spirituality, 35–36, 41
    imperialism, 181
    integration in, 105
    life, 103–4
    parochialism, 181
    pollution, 53, 55, 57

sensitivity in the Third World, 193
"worldly," 106
Sri Lanka, 126, 151
Stam, J., 79, 83
Substantialist categories, 183
Sumithra, S., 31, 130–32
Symbols, 129
Syncretism, 28
Sudanic Civilization, 15
Suzuki, D. T., 142

Taoism, 121, 124, 136, 142
Takenaka, M., 145, 146
Taylor, C., 21, 117
Taylor, J. V., 59, 70
Technology, 19
Thek (respect in Neur language), 53
Theology, theological,
  Asian, 121–62
  Chinese, 135–41
  Christocentric, 135
  concepts, 188
  concrete orientation in, 189
  contextualized, 29–31
  cross-cultural, 20, 24
  functional, 90
  interactional model of, 29
  method, 91
  missions and, 189
  regional, 19
  traditional, 41
  translation model of, 22, 17
  universal, 196
  Western, 20, 23, 86
Theology and Praxis (C. Boff), 114, 115
A Theology of Liberation (G. Gutiérrez), 80–81
Theological Pitfalls in Africa (B. Kato), 64
Theory and practice. *See* Praxis.
Things Fall Apart (C. Achebe), 40
Third World,
  defined, 14–16

and Evangelicalism, 17–20
hope and, 190
rise of, 11–14
Third World Ecumenical Association, 14
Thomas, M. M., 29, 129, 130
Thompson, P. E. S., 61
Tibet, 124, 127
Tienou, T., 58
Time (in African religion), 61
Torres, S., 50, 64
Tracy, D., 191
Traditional values, 124
Transformation, 29
Transphenomenal reality, 125
Trinity, 58
Truth, 100
Tutu, D., 69

Uhuru (freedom), 39
Ujamaa (Tanzanian socialism), 50
Underdevelopment, 84
Union Seminary (India), 131
Unionism, 99
Universal theology. *See* Theology.
Unity and diversity in Christology. *See* Christology.
Universalism, 64
Upanishads, 122
Urbanization, 72, 118

Values, 29, 31, 33
  African, 68
  cultural, 42
  indigenous, 192
Vatican II, 79–80, 99
Vedanta, 131
Venkaya (Indian untouchable), 24–29, 32, 33, 187
Verkuyl, J., 189
Vietnam, 138
Violence, 92–93
Vishnu, 140
Volf, M., 116

INDEX

von Ranke, L., 84

Walls, A. F., 13, 19
Waterbuffalo Theology (K. Koyama), 146
We Drink From Our Own Wells (G. Gutiérrez), 105
Weerasingha, T., 133
West Bank, 12
Western world, 19, 38, 89, 126, 128
  thought patterns, 131
WHO/FAO (United Nations), 14
White, R., 83
Wood, C., 189
Word of God, 100, 103

Work of Christ, 184
World Christian, 185–86
World War II, 12, 19

Xavier, F., 141
Xenocentrism, 20

Yin and yang, 140
Yoga, 127
Yoruba tribe (Africa), 47

Zen Buddhism, 142
Ziegenbalg, B., 125, 126
Zimbabwe, 36
Zuesse, E., 43, 49–50, 52

Learning About Theology was typeset by the
Photocomposition Department of Zondervan Publishing House,
Grand Rapids, Michigan on a Mergenthaler Linotron 202/N.
Compositor: Susan A. Koppenol
Editor: Gerard Terpstra

*The text was set in 10 point Times Roman, a face
designed by Stanley Morison in 1931 for the London
Times. Times Roman is compact, economical, and popular
for bookwork. This book was printed on 50-pound Husky
Vellum paper by Color House Graphics,
Grand Rapids, Michigan.*